God's Saving Love

*Gospel Images
for Prayer*

JOHN

by Robert L. Knopp

Foreword by Robert F. Morneau

Pauline
BOOKS & MEDIA

Nihil Obstat:
Rev. Thomas W. Buckley, STD, SSL

Imprimatur:
†Bernard Cardinal Law
Archbishop of Boston
June 10, 1996

Cover design: Sergia Ballini, FSP

ISBN 0-8198-3088-7

Printed and published in the U.S.A. by Pauline Books & Media, 50 Saint Pauls Avenue, Boston MA 02130-3491.

http://www.pauline.org

Pauline Books & Media is the publishing house of the Daughters of St. Paul, an international congregation of women religious serving the Church with the communications media.

1 2 3 4 5 6   03 02 01 00 99 98

Contents

Foreword

A fierce battle is taking place in our culture regarding the imagination. Nor is this a *cold* war but one of extreme passion and intensity. The importance of victory cannot be exaggerated because the images we create or absorb shape our inner attitudes, which in turn radically influence our lifestyle and behavior. It's a simple syllogism but one which has profound ramifications.

Images come from multiple sources: television, songs, movies, magazines, science, poetry, lived lives. Within the Christian community a major source stimulating the imagination is sacred Scripture. God's word often draws pictures for us that contain values and virtues that lead us to the kingdom: Jesus as good shepherd; our spirituality as one of mutual self-giving as depicted in the vine and the branches; the separation of the sheep and the goats based on our treatment of one another; God as the potter shaping and molding our lives.

In a world filled with incredible violence, the Christian community continues to offer an alternative to the culture of death. Ours is to be a culture of love, a "civilization of love," in which every single human being is invited to the wedding feast and must be treated with awesome respect. The poet Gerard Manley Hopkins calls us "immortal diamonds." Our images must offer realistic hope.

It is not enough to encounter an image, symbol, metaphor or story. More is required. We must assimilate and appropriate these formative sights and sounds until they are absorbed into our spiritual bloodstream. This will require prayer and reflection as well as commitment to translate them into action. Our process of formation and conversion takes time and much grace. Perseverance in prayer is essential to Christian maturity.

This volume, like its three companions, is about discipleship and how we respond to that call by using biblical images. Robert Knopp looks deeply into each of the Gospels and extracts for us images that give us access to the person of Jesus. Each Gospel is unique in its approach to the Lord but all are the same in inviting us to know, love and serve him with all of our being.

In *God's Saving Love*, we encounter the great mystery of the incarnation, God-become-man. Jesus, the Word of God enfleshed, draws us into deep mystery and teaches us of the profound love of God. The Jesus in John's Gospel is noble, solemn, kingly. We are given an insight into his humanity by means of his divinity. Through prayer and meditation we hopefully will be able to exclaim: "My Lord and my God!"

One last word about images, the cornerstone of this book. Flannery O'Connor, in her collection of essays *Mystery and Manners*, writes: "The isolated imagination is easily corrupted in theory, but the writer inside his community seldom has such a problem." St. John was deep inside the community, yes, inside the community of the Trinity. Thus we are given an incredible glimpse into the mystery of our God.

+Robert F. Morneau
Auxiliary Bishop of Green Bay

Invitation

This small book joins its predecessors—*Mark: A Very Human Jesus, Matthew: Our Healing God-With-Us,* and *Luke: Our Compassionate Savior*—to complete the series of *Gospel Images for Prayer.* In this series I reflect upon the images by which each evangelist presents Jesus and his message, moving our minds to believe and our hearts to love and pray. After teaching *about* the Gospels for many years, I simply had to try to enter more directly *into each Gospel*—to live it, breathe it and pray it, as Vatican II urges us:

> Learn by frequent reading of the divine Scriptures the "excellent knowledge of Jesus Christ" (Phil 3:8).... Prayer should accompany the reading of sacred Scripture, so that God and man may talk together; for "we speak to him when we pray; we hear him when we read the divine sayings" (*Dogmatic Constitution on Divine Revelation,* no. 25, quoting St. Ambrose).

According to ancient tradition John's was the last Gospel to be written. Modern scholars add that it was probably not John himself but one or more members of his "school" who wrote it, using John's eyewitness data and profiting by his long life of meditation upon Jesus and his message.

The result is the most insightful of the Gospels, much different from the first three in both content and style. These first three, the synoptic Gospels, are especially rich in images. These are not primarily the sentient images that appeal to our imagination through color, form and sound, but action images that invite us through narratives and parables to explore the spiritual sense, the inner mystery of Jesus. John uses this same kind of imagery but often with a higher degree of symbolism, more characteristic of poetry. He loves to play on such words as "word" itself in contrast to the *"Word"*—his "word of God" explodes into "the Word was God." He awakens us with the similar play of "light" and *"Light"* and sharp contrasts between "light" and "darkness," "spirit" and "flesh," "born of woman" and "born from above," "water" and "living water," "bread" and "bread of heaven." These word-plays reach far beyond fancy. They propel us intuitively from our temporal world into the ethereal reaches of God's eternal world of spirit that John considers *the real world,* only faintly reflected in ours of matter, time and space. His symbolic language suggests breathtaking insights into the meaning of our lives in relation to God's life.

In John, even Jesus' actions become symbols, signs indicating who he really is, signs flashing with insights into the inner mystery of his being. John uses narratives, but instead of parables, his Jesus speaks more directly than in the synoptics. He teaches about our relationship with God, while speaking of his own relationship with his Father. The mystery of Jesus is revealed in John's narrative "signs" of Jesus' identity and reports of his teachings. To penetrate progressively into this mystery, I have divided John's Gospel into units in which a key insight or cluster of insights can stir our musing and prayer. Then in simple, rhythmic sense lines intended to harmonize with John's eloquently simple language and poetic tone, I reflect on these insights until they lead us into prayer.

In his prologue, John establishes the identity of Jesus Christ as the *Word* of God made flesh—the incarnate Word. Although John does not later repeat this identification, it casts light on his more common naming of Jesus as "Son of God," and it lies beneath the profound words John attributes to Jesus. Far different from his speech in the synoptics, Jesus speaks in John with the supreme solemnity of the Word through whom and for whom God created the world (Col 1:16), the Son who with his Father sends us the Holy Spirit, revealing the Triune God himself.

By presenting Jesus as God-become-man, John shows us the saving love of a God who sends his only Son to become one of us. John then focuses on Jesus' humanity in the light of his divinity. Even in his passion, John's Jesus conducts himself with a nobility muted in the other Gospels—a kingliness, a godliness, consistent with the image of Jesus as the Word of God enfleshed. This key image of God-become-man reaches climactic clarity in Thomas' bold proclamation: "My Lord and my God!" Jesus is God-become-man—the God who not only transcends his creation but enters into it with his saving love, to share our very lives and share his life with us.

Even more than the others, this fourth Gospel seems to have been written with a catechetical intention. What better way of presenting the truth about the Father, the Son, and the Spirit than in words of Jesus, the revealing Word? The writer often uses the question and answer technique that became the classic form of catechesis. In the first Johannine conversation, for example, Nicodemus asks Jesus a question about salvation and Jesus answers. But Nicodemus misunderstands his answer and asks a further question, which Jesus answers on a deeper level. And so go the conversations with the Samaritan woman and his disciples, in questions and answers that probe ever deeper into the mystery of the God who has become one of us—and from this vantage point within our race offers us a share in his own eternal life.

Awareness of John's basic catechetical form enables us to read his Gospel with greater understanding. Two other principles are also helpful in our efforts to understand and appreciate Scripture. First, we must read in context—in the immediate context of John's Gospel and Letters and in the overall context of Scripture—according to our faith that the Holy Spirit inspired all the biblical writers and does not contradict himself, despite any appearances to the contrary. Second, we must keep in mind the general purpose of all sacred Scripture: to reveal the absolute goodness of the God whom the First Letter of John defines as "Love" (4:8).

In *The Life of Moses*, Gregory of Nyssa offers a powerful corollary to these principles: "Anything in sacred Scripture that in its literal sense would be unworthy of God must have some hidden inner meaning." This concept evidently applies also to the evangelists' efforts to present Jesus. Thus, when John quotes him as saying, "I came into this world...so that those who do not see may see, and those who do see may become blind" (Jn 9:39), we must not understand him as literally telling us that he came to make people blind. He is emphasizing figuratively that certain Pharisees, by their narrow

adherence to the sabbath law, had blinded themselves to his great miracle of giving sight to a man
born blind (cf. Jn 9:1-38).

In the relatively few passages over which
Christian churches still differ, I have adhered to the
Catholic Church's interpretation of the apostolic
traditions that gave rise to the New Testament.
Though the Church has rarely interpreted indi-
vidual verses, it provides an overall understanding
of Scripture through the kerygma and its corollary
doctrines, roughed out by the apostles themselves
(as suggested in Acts 15 and some later passages of
the New Testament, such as 2 Pt 1:16-21 and 3:16),
and refined by the early Fathers of the Church and
the councils.

I lovingly dedicate this book to my wife
Marian, always the dearest partisan of my efforts.

Now enter with me into John's Gospel to pon-
der and pray over one insight or group of insights
each day. Do not let John's deep beginning discour-
age you; take his apparent conundrums as his challenge to enter with him into the depths of God's
very life—depths he will gradually clarify as we
proceed through his Gospel. May these lines help
us find with him the Jesus who is the very Word of
God living in us with his Spirit, to be our light on
our way to the God he reveals as his Father—and
ours.

Prologue
and the
Book of Signs

The Word *Was with God....*
The Word *Was God*

John 1:1-3: *In the beginning was the Word, and the Word was with God, and the Word was God. He was in the beginning with God. All things came into being through him, and without him not one thing came into being.*

To contemplate:

John, you raise more questions than you resolve.
  In the beginning of *what?*
And how can the Word be with your God—
  and yet be *God himself?*

Does your first phrase echo Genesis
  to add an inner meaning
to God's creation of our world
  of nature and human beings?

God works through his creating word:
  "Let there be light....!"
His word is his creative power—
  no sooner said than done.

And so his word is more than word,
    and more than figure of speech—
more than Wisdom personified,
    playing within God's work (Prov 8:22-31).

God's Word, like ours, is *with* himself,
    yet *is* his very self!
God, pure spirit, beyond all matter,
    communicates himself.

His Word, you hint, is personal,
    a Person with the speaker,
a Person with God's very power—
    a Person who is God.

O mystery of mysteries!
    You glimpse the life of God
to faintly trace the secret truth
    that lies beyond our world.

Without God's Word, nothing was;
    without him, nothing is.
    O Word of God, be praised!

The Word Collaborated
in Our Creation

Jn 1:3-5: *What has come into being in him [God's Word] was life, and the life was the light of all people. The light shines in the darkness, and the darkness did not overcome it.*

To contemplate:

John, you interpret God's great work
    in the Genesis account;
you deepen Proverbs' deep reflection,
    beyond all human reason.

On his first workday God made the light;
    he made it by his word.
So through his Word who is his Light,
    our light reflects his Light.

The Word of God is more than word—
    lives God's very life.
The Light of God is more than light—
    brightens our own poor life.

God made a dome to divide the waters,
    made earth and vegetation;
he made the sun and moon and stars,
    made animals and fish.

And last of all, he made human life
    in the image of himself.
Yet his Word is his own perfect image (Col 1:15)—
    his Word lives his very life.

His Word shares that life with us
    as images of God.
We men and women live in real light,
    when we live in the light of his Word.

Failing this, we die in darkness,
    the darkness the light dispels.
If we live in Christ, we live in light,
    the light that is God's own life.

O John, your view of God's inner world
    delves deep beyond our ken.
O God of life and brightest light,
    let your Word light up our lives!

The True Light Is Jesus Christ

Jn 1:6-13: *There was a man sent from God, whose name was John. He came as a witness to testify to the light, so that all might believe through him. He himself was not the light, but he came to testify to the light. The true light, which enlightens everyone, was coming into the world.*

He was in the world, and the world came into being through him; yet the world did not know him. He came to what was his own, and his own people did not accept him. But to all who received him, who believed in his name, he gave power to become children of God, who were born, not of blood or of the will of the flesh or of the will of man, but of God.

To contemplate:

John's brief history of the world
    now jumps to another John,
God's messenger sent to tell his people
    of the coming of his light.

Though some had thought this John was light,
    he was only the lowly herald
of the light who would teach us all the truth
    to light our way to God.

This Word of God who was God's light
    in his creative work,
now entered into our dark world—
    entered as one of us.

He lived among the men he'd made,
    lived and worked with them;
yet they knew him not nor understood
    the words he said to them.

He was the very Word of God,
    but his word was lost to them;
he was the very Light of God,
    but some preferred the dark.

To those who believed his word to them
    and received him in their hearts
he gave new life in his own full life—
    sons and daughters of God.

They were born again, remade in him,
    in the Image of our God.
    O Word, be born in us!

The Word Became Flesh

Jn 1:14-15: *And the Word became flesh and lived among us, and we have seen his glory, the glory as of a father's only son, full of grace and truth. (John testified to him and cried out, "This was he of whom I said, 'He who comes after me ranks ahead of me because he was before me.'")*

To contemplate:

God speaks forth his living Word,
   alive with his own life;
and through his Word God made our world,
   made us in his light.

And then his Word became our flesh,
   a man like one of us.
God's Word, says John, is that same child
   who is the son of Mary.

Before he became human like us,
   he was the Son of God,
Word and Son of his Father-God,
   full of grace and truth.

Of him John the Baptist testified:
    "I am indeed unworthy
even to untie the thong of his sandals (1:27)—
    he ranks far ahead of me."

"He comes after me, yet ranks ahead,
    because he was before me.
Yes, he lived before God made the world,
    lived the life of God."

Yet down from his Father's glory-throne
    he leaped to our world below—
into the womb of Blessed Mary
    to take of her flesh his own.

The Word-made-flesh is Jesus Christ,
    the light of all the world;
the Word-made-flesh is one of us,
    a human being with us.

O Son of God and son of Mary,
    share your life with me!

The Son Has Revealed His Father

Jn 1:16-18: *From his fullness we have all received, grace upon grace. The law indeed was given through Moses; grace and truth came through Jesus Christ. No one has ever seen God. It is God the only Son, who is close to the Father's heart, who has made him known.*

To contemplate:

Whatever gifts of grace we have,
    we owe to Jesus Christ.
Whatever light and life we have,
    is his pure gift to us.

For he possesses all the grace
    his Father reserves for us.
Moses gave us God's pure law;
    Jesus gives his life.

Moses glimpsed God on the mount,
    received his law in stone;
Jesus sees God face to face,
    receives his love as Son.

That love he relays out to us,
    the love of a Father's heart;
for he reveals our God to us
    as our loving Father-God.

No other man has known our God
    as Jesus Christ has known him—
not Buddha, Confucius or Mohammed;
    not even great Abraham
    knew God as his own Father.

Thus, John, you begin your Gospel,
    right from the very beginning,
in which the Word of God took part
    with the Father of creation.

This Word, who became a man for us
    and spoke the word of God,
Is our own Lord, our Jesus Christ,
    the Father's Son-with-us.

O Jesus Christ, our Father's Son,
    reveal God's heart to us!

Make Straight the Way of the Lord

Jn 1:19-28: *This is the testimony given by John when the Jews sent priests and Levites from Jerusalem to ask him, "Who are you?" He confessed and did not deny it, but confessed, "I am not the Messiah." And they asked him, "What then? Are you Elijah?" He said, "I am not." "Are you the prophet?" He answered, "No." Then they said to him, "Who are you? Let us have an answer for those who sent us. What do you say about yourself?" He said,*

"I am the voice of one crying out in the wilderness,
'Make straight the way of the Lord,'"
as the prophet Isaiah said.

Now they had been sent from the Pharisees. They asked him, "Why then are you baptizing if you are neither the Messiah, nor Elijah, nor the prophet?" John answered them, "I baptize with water. Among you stands one whom you do not know, the one who is coming after me; I am not worthy to untie the thong of his sandal." This took place in Bethany across the Jordan where John was baptizing.

To contemplate:

John the Baptist, from out the desert,
  is a voice of bygone ages—
    a voice that no one hears.

Yet he still cries out,
  his message clear,
    a message no one *wants* to hear!

From far-off Jerusalem they come,
  the Pharisees' messengers,
    to test God's messenger.

Of course, he does not pass the test.
  How could a voice in the wilderness
    tell God's holy truth?

How could the voice of such a man
  teach even the Pharisees?
    Who, indeed, is John?

Out of nowhere he has appeared,
  no training his, no ancestry
    to impress Israel's elite.

Yet, John, I believe you speak the truth
  about the world's Messiah.
    Jesus, I believe in you—
      come straight into my heart!

The Holy Spirit Remains with Jesus

Jn 1:29-34: *The next day he saw Jesus coming toward him and declared, "Here is the Lamb of God who takes away the sin of the world! This is he of whom I said, 'After me comes a man who ranks ahead of me because he was before me.' I myself did not know him; but I came baptizing with water for this reason, that he might be revealed to Israel." And John testified, "I saw the Spirit descending from heaven like a dove, and it remained on him. I myself did not know him, but the one who sent me to baptize with water said to me, 'He on whom you see the Spirit descend and remain is the one who baptizes with the Holy Spirit.' And I myself have seen and have testified that this is the Son of God."*

To contemplate:

John the Baptist, God's visionary,
　　sees the Spirit descend on Jesus:
God's clear sign to identify
　　Jesus as his own pure Lamb—
unblemished lamb of sacrifice,
　　whose blood will save his people,

whose flesh will feed his people
   in memory of deliverance (Ex 12:5-14);
Lamb that Isaiah prophesied
   would be God's faithful servant,
"crushed for our iniquities,"
   slaughtered for our sins (Is 53:5-7).

This Lamb of God, led by the Spirit,
   is the very Son of God,
obedient to his Father's will
   to give us the Spirit, too.

How do we really think of God?
   As deliverer from enemies (Ex 3:7 ff.),
as guiding pillar of cloud and fire (Ex 13:21-22),
   as bearing us on eagle's wings (Ex 19:4)?
Look at the God John here presents:
   a Father who sends us his only Son,
   a Son who is a gentle Lamb,
   a Spirit who is a peaceful Dove.

O Father, thanks for sending your Son
   to bear our sins in death.
O Son, gentle Lamb of God,
   thanks for sending your Spirit.
O Holy Spirit, peaceful Dove,
   hover over us!

Come and See

Jn 1:35-42: *The next day John again was standing with two of his disciples, and as he watched Jesus walk by, he exclaimed, "Look, here is the Lamb of God!" The two disciples heard him say this, and they followed Jesus. When Jesus turned and saw them following, he said to them, "What are you looking for?" They said to him, "Rabbi" (which translated means Teacher), "where are you staying?" He said to them, "Come and see." They came and saw where he was staying, and they remained with him that day. It was about four o'clock in the afternoon. One of the two who heard John speak and followed him was Andrew, Simon Peter's brother. He first found his brother Simon and said to him, "We have found the Messiah" (which is translated Anointed). He brought Simon to Jesus, who looked at him and said, "You are Simon son of John. You are to be called Cephas" (which is translated Peter).*

To contemplate:

"What are you looking for in life?"
  Money to give you ease?
Pleasure to slake your heart's desire?
  Power to dominate others?

"We're looking for the Lamb of God
  who will teach us the way to life.
O Lamb of God, where do you live?
  For we would live with you."

"Come with me and you will see—
  you must stay with me."

One day, one single day they need
  to be thoroughly convinced
that he is who John said he is—
  the very Lamb of God.

Then Andrew seeks his brother Simon:
  "We've found God's Anointed One!"
John has been Jesus' first recruiter;
  Andrew, his second one.

A glance, and Jesus knows his man:
  "Simon, son of John are you,
but I now rename you Peter,
  and call you to be my rock."

O Jesus, gentle Lamb of God,
  I, too, would live with you!

Follow Me

Jn 1:43-51: *The next day Jesus decided to go to Galilee. He found Philip and said to him, "Follow me." Now Philip was from Bethsaida, the city of Andrew and Peter. Philip found Nathanael and said to him, "We have found him about whom Moses in the law and also the prophets wrote, Jesus son of Joseph from Nazareth." Nathanael said to him, "Can anything good come out of Nazareth?" Philip said to him, "Come and see." When Jesus saw Nathanael coming toward him, he said of him, "Here is truly an Israelite in whom there is no deceit!" Nathanael asked him, "Where did you get to know me?" Jesus answered, "I saw you under the fig tree before Philip called you." Nathanael replied, "Rabbi, you are the Son of God! You are the King of Israel!" Jesus answered, "Do you believe because I told you that I saw you under the fig tree? You will see greater things than these." And he said to him, "Very truly, I tell you, you will see heaven opened and the angels of God ascending and descending upon the Son of Man."*

To contemplate:

Five recruits has Jesus now;
  each new disciple finds another,
    and thus they multiply.

Jesus knows the men he calls,
  more than they know themselves—
    knows their inner souls.

Nathanael knows of Nazareth,
  that no good comes from there—
    yet Jesus breaks his bias.

For Jesus knows some incident
  by which he proved his worth;
    Nathanael stands in awe.

If Jesus could know so much of him,
  he must be the Son of God
    and King of Israel!

"So easily convinced, Nathanael?
  You'll see more than Jacob saw,
    when heaven opened to him" (Gen 28:12).

O Jesus, Son of God and Israel's king,
  you who open heaven to all,
    I, too, would follow you!

Do Whatever He Tells You

Jn 2:1-5: *On the third day there was a wedding in Cana of Galilee, and the mother of Jesus was there. Jesus and his disciples had also been invited to the wedding. When the wine gave out, the mother of Jesus said to him, "They have no wine." And Jesus said to her, "Woman, what concern is that to you and to me? My hour has not yet come." His mother said to the servants, "Do whatever he tells you."*

To contemplate:

"And the mother of Jesus was there."
What kind of person was Jesus' mother?

One who first was truly a woman—
the word Jesus used to address her.

A woman who was a loyal friend—
she'd been invited to the wedding feast.

A woman who worked behind the scenes—
she was first to know the wine gave out.

A woman who cared for other's needs—
she spared the couple embarrassment.

The woman who knew her son's great power—
when the wine gave out she went to him.

The woman who knew her son's great heart—
she saw through his seeming negative.

The woman who knew the heart of God—
she knew the hour that God had set.

The woman who could take charge of others—
she told the servants: "Do what he says."

O woman, come into our lives, too;
take charge behind the outward scene.

O Mary, stand by us when we're sad:
tell your son, "They lack wine of joy."
O Mary, be with us when we're tempted:
tell your son, "They need wine of grace."
O Mary, be always at our side
to remind us to do "whatever he says."

The First of Jesus' Signs

Jn 2:6-12: *Now standing there were six stone water jars for the Jewish rites of purification, each holding twenty or thirty gallons. Jesus said to them, "Fill the jars with water." And they filled them up to the brim. He said to them, "Now draw some out, and take it to the chief steward." So they took it. When the steward tasted the water that had become wine, and did not know where it came from (though the servants who had drawn the water knew), the steward called the bridegroom and said to him, "Everyone serves the good wine first, and then the inferior wine after the guests have become drunk. But you have kept the good wine until now." Jesus did this, the first of his signs, in Cana of Galilee, and revealed his glory; and his disciples believed in him.*

After this he went down to Capernaum with his mother, his brothers, and his disciples; and they remained there a few days.

To contemplate:

She had not seen him work a wonder;
    yet when the wine gave out,
she knew whom to ask for help—
    her own dear, loving son.

And the miracle he then did work
    was such a generous one,
it gave his disciples a clear sign
    of who he really was.

And it gave a hint of a future gift:
    If he could change mere water
into the richest wine of all,
    why not wine to blood—
    his own precious blood?

And thus he blessed a marriage feast,
    blessed the wedding pair—
made marriage vows most holy
    in his own sacred presence.

Jesus begins his public life,
    answering his mother's prayer.
She walks with him to Capernaum,
    his center in Galilee.

O Mary, walk along with us,
    as we walk on Jesus' way.
O Jesus, turn our water to wine—
    our family life to bliss.

Jesus' Zeal for God's House

Jn 2:13-22: The Passover of the Jews was near, and Jesus went up to Jerusalem. In the temple he found people selling cattle, sheep, and doves, and the money changers seated at their tables. Making a whip of cords, he drove all of them out of the temple, both the sheep and the cattle. He also poured out the coins of the money changers and overturned their tables. He told those who were selling the doves, "Take these things out of here! Stop making my Father's house a marketplace!" His disciples remembered that it was written, "Zeal for your house will consume me." The Jews then said to him, "What sign can you show us for doing this?" Jesus answered them, "Destroy this temple, and in three days I will raise it up." The Jews then said, "This temple has been under construction for forty-six years, and will you raise it up in three days?" But he was speaking of the temple of his body. After he was raised from the dead, his disciples remembered that he had said this; and they believed the scripture and the word that Jesus had spoken.

To contemplate:

Having blessed a joyful marriage feast,
   Jesus goes up to Jerusalem
to celebrate the Passover feast;
   but his joy turns into anger.

He drives the cattle merchants out,
   spills money changers' coins;
even the sellers of gentle doves
   he severely reprimands.

His disciples recall the psalmist's word,
   "Zeal for your house consumes me" (Ps 69:9).
Yes, he will be consumed indeed—
   the temple of his body.

He'll give his life to prove his point:
   "This is my Father's house!
Keep pure the worship of our God,
   adoration of my Father."

O Jesus, we lose our lives in things,
   spend them to buy and sell;
we leave no room for God to dwell
   within our busy lives!

O Jesus, drive all passing things
   out of my crowded mind;
drive all love of false desires
   from my chaotic heart.

You Must Be Born from Above

Jn 3:1-10: *Now there was a Pharisee named Nicodemus, a leader of the Jews. He came to Jesus by night and said to him, "Rabbi, we know that you are a teacher who has come from God; for no one can do these signs that you do apart from the presence of God." Jesus answered him, "Very truly, I tell you, no one can see the kingdom of God without being born from above." Nicodemus said to him, "How can anyone be born after having grown old? Can one enter a second time into the mother's womb and be born?" Jesus answered, "Very truly, I tell you, no one can enter the kingdom of God without being born of water and Spirit. What is born of the flesh is flesh, and what is born of the Spirit is spirit. Do not be astonished that I said to you, 'You must be born from above.' The wind blows where it chooses, and you hear the sound of it, but you do not know where it comes from or where it goes. So it is with everyone who is born of the Spirit." Nicodemus said to him, "How can these things be?" Jesus answered, "Are you a teacher of Israel, and yet you do not understand these things?"*

To contemplate:

Nicodemus, teacher of Israel,
  comes in search of answers;
he believes Jesus comes from God—
  Jesus knows the answers.

God's kingdom is a spirit-world
  beyond all flesh and blood.
No one can know this spirit-world,
  until reborn from above.

Born again—not of mere flesh—
  born of the Holy Spirit,
in Baptism that brings the Spirit-God
  into our inner life.

More mysterious than the wind,
  the Spirit comes and goes;
for the Spirit is the breath of God
  into our very soul (Gen 2:7).

Only the man who comes from God
  can tell us such great things;
only the man who comes from God
  can bring us his Holy Spirit.

O mystery-Spirit from above,
  O wind of the God of love,
come, move our minds and hearts to love—
  fill them with *your Love!*

God So Loved the World

Jn 3:11-21: *"Very truly, I tell you, we speak of what we know and testify to what we have seen; yet you do not receive our testimony. If I have told you about earthly things and you do not believe, how can you believe if I tell you about heavenly things? No one has ascended into heaven except the one who descended from heaven, the Son of Man. And just as Moses lifted up the serpent in the wilderness, so must the Son of Man be lifted up, that whoever believes in him may have eternal life.*

"For God so loved the world that he gave his only Son, so that everyone who believes in him may not perish but may have eternal life.

"Indeed, God did not send the Son into the world to condemn the world, but in order that the world might be saved through him. Those who believe in him are not condemned; but those who do not believe are condemned already, because they have not believed in the name of the only Son of God. And this is the judgment, that the light has come into the world, and people loved darkness rather than light because their deeds were evil. For all who do evil hate the light and do not come to the light, so that their deeds may not be exposed. But those who do

what is true come to the light, so that it may be clearly seen that their deeds have been done in God."

To contemplate:

In the desert Moses healed the people
   of the venom of biting snakes,
by raising high upon a pole
   the figure of a snake (Num 21:9).

Just so, the Son of Man, raised up,
   heals us of our sin;
condemned as traitor to his people,
   his death is death to our sins.

For he is the only Son of God,
   who gives him to our world,
that in him we be lifted up
   into God's own realm.

Though we deserve God's condemnation,
   he sends us his only Son
to answer for our grave transgressions
   and save us from ourselves.

O God of Jesus, God of Love,
   how could you so love us
as to give your Son's very life for us—
   how could you love us so?

   God, may we love you so!

He Must Increase; I Must Decrease

Jn 3:22-30: *After this Jesus and his disciples went into the Judean countryside, and he spent some time there with them and baptized....*

Now a discussion about purification arose between John's disciples and a Jew. They came to John and said to him, "Rabbi, the one who was with you across the Jordan, to whom you testified, here he is baptizing, and all are going to him." John answered, "No one can receive anything except what has been given from heaven. You yourselves are my witnesses that I said, 'I am not the Messiah, but I have been sent ahead of him.' He who has the bride is the bridegroom. The friend of the bridegroom, who stands and hears him, rejoices greatly at the bridegroom's voice. For this reason my joy has been fulfilled. He must increase, but I must decrease."

To contemplate:

God has given John his gift
   as the great Messiah's herald;
like the best man at a marriage rite,
   John stands there by the groom.

O John, teach us to esteem our gifts
in true humility.
Teach us to rejoice in the groom
who alone can have the bride.

John brings his flock to Jesus,
not to himself as groom.
We must give praise to Jesus,
not glorify ourselves.

For Jesus alone can be the groom
foretold in ancient times (Is 62:5);
Jesus alone can speak for God
as bridegroom of his people.

Therefore John must disappear
to make room for the rightful groom;
his work now done, John fades away
as Jesus forward comes.

Model of all evangelizers,
John knows his rightful place.
John, teach us to be more like you
in serving our true bridegroom!
O Jesus, increase your life in me,
as my own life declines.

Who Believes in the Son
Has Eternal Life

Jn 3:31-36: *The one who comes from above is above all; the one who is of the earth belongs to the earth and speaks about earthly things. The one who comes from heaven is above all. He testifies to what he has seen and heard, yet no one accepts his testimony. Whoever has accepted his testimony, has certified this, that God is true. He whom God has sent speaks the words of God, for he gives the Spirit without measure. The Father loves the Son and has placed all things in his hands. Whoever believes in the Son has eternal life; whoever disobeys the Son will not see life, but must endure God's wrath.*

To contemplate:

Here John recapitulates
   the beginning of his book—
reflections deeper than the sea,
   more expansive than continents.

Jesus alone is from above;
   he alone knows God.
Only Jesus can speak for God;
   yet no one seems to hear.

Those who hear what Jesus says
    know that God is true—
so true to the world that he has made,
    he loves it as his own,

for he has sent his only Son
    to save it from disaster,
the catastrophe of sinking back
    into primal nothingness.

The creating wind he sent of old (Gen 1:2),
    he sends now yet again;
the wind that is the Holy Spirit,
    his Son now brings once more:

God bestows on us beyond all measure
    the Spirit of his Son,
the Spirit who restores all things,
    prepares for eternal life.

O Jesus, I do believe in you
    as bridegroom of us all.
Send me your Spirit from above;
    renew my soul in love!

Jesus Offers Living Water

Jn 4:1-15: *Now when Jesus learned that the Pharisees had heard, "Jesus is making and baptizing more disciples than John"—although it was not Jesus himself but his disciples who baptized—he left Judea and started back to Galilee. But he had to go through Samaria. So he came to a Samaritan city called Sychar, near the plot of ground that Jacob had given to his son Joseph. Jacob's well was there, and Jesus, tired out by his journey, was sitting by the well. It was about noon.*

A Samaritan woman came to draw water, and Jesus said to her, "Give me a drink." (His disciples had gone to the city to buy food.) The Samaritan woman said to him, "How is it that you, a Jew, ask a drink of me, a woman of Samaria?" (Jews do not share things in common with Samaritans.) Jesus answered her, "If you knew the gift of God, and who it is that is saying to you, 'Give me a drink,' you would have asked him, and he would have given you living water." The woman said to him, "Sir, you have no bucket, and the well is deep. Where do you get that living water? Are you greater than our ancestor Jacob, who gave us the well, and with his sons and his flocks drank from it?" Jesus said to her, "Everyone who drinks of this water will be thirsty again, but those who drink of the water that I will give them will never be thirsty. The water that I will give will become in them a spring of water gushing up to eternal life." The woman said to him, "Sir, give me this water, so that I may never be thirsty or have to keep coming here to draw water."

To contemplate:

Much greater than our father Jacob,
    this Jesus sitting here
by Jacob's well and asking a woman
    for a simple drink of water.

How could he, a man of Israel,
    ask this favor of a woman?
How could he, of Jacob's line,
    ask a Samaritan anything?
He has no pride, this Son of God,
    no pride of sex or race;
he does not even own a bucket
    to draw water from a well.

Yet he speaks of living water,
    greater than from this well
that father Jacob left his sons
    and people of Samaria.

O Jesus, give me your living water;
    I'm not too proud to ask,
for I believe your every word—
    you speak the word of God!

I Am the Messiah

Jn 4:16-26: *Jesus said to her, "Go, call your husband, and come back." The woman answered him, "I have no husband." Jesus said to her, "You are right in saying, 'I have no husband'; for you have had five husbands, and the one you have now is not your husband. What you have said is true!" The woman said to him, "Sir, I see that you are a prophet. Our ancestors worshiped on this mountain, but you say that the place where people must worship is in Jerusalem." Jesus said to her, "Woman, believe me, the hour is coming when you will worship the Father neither on this mountain nor in Jerusalem. You worship what you do not know; we worship what we know, for salvation is from the Jews. But the hour is coming, and is now here, when the true worshipers will worship the Father in spirit and truth, for the Father seeks such as these to worship him. God is spirit, and those who worship him must worship in spirit and truth." The woman said to him, "I know that Messiah is coming" (who is called Christ). "When he comes, he will proclaim all things to us." Jesus said to her, "I am he, the one who is speaking to you."*

To contemplate:

He looks into the woman's heart,
   knows her present and her past,
moves her to see her emptiness,
   her desperate need of him.

She responds with simple truthfulness,
   asks to know more truth—
the truth about her God himself,
   how best to worship him.

"Turn the way the Spirit leads,
   accept the true Messiah,
and worship God the way he says—
   God of spirit and truth."

"And who is this Messiah, sir?"
   "It is he who speaks with you!"
This thunderbolt from his sacred lips
   tests her faith and mine.

O Jesus, I do believe in you,
   my own Anointed Lord!
Open my heart to the Spirit's word
   who guides me to the truth.

My Food Is to Do My Father's Will

Jn 4:27-38: *Just then his disciples came. They were astonished that he was speaking with a woman, but no one said, "What do you want?" or, "Why are you speaking with her?" Then the woman left her water jar and went back to the city. She said to the people, "Come and see a man who told me everything I have ever done! He cannot be the Messiah, can he?" They left the city and were on their way to him.*

Meanwhile the disciples were urging him, "Rabbi, eat something." But he said to them, "I have food to eat that you do not know about." So the disciples said to one another, "Surely no one has brought him something to eat?" Jesus said to them, "My food is to do the will of him who sent me and to complete his work. Do you not say, 'Four months more, then comes the harvest'? But I tell you, look around you, and see how the fields are ripe for harvesting. The reaper is already receiving wages and is gathering fruit for eternal life, so that sower and reaper may rejoice together. For here the saying holds true, 'One sows and another reaps.' I sent you to reap that for which you did not labor. Others have labored, and you have entered into their labor."

To contemplate:

Jesus has sown the seed of truth,
  even in Samaria;
he needs no other food for strength
  than to do his Father's will.

Though the fields are not ready yet
  for the reapers' sharpened scythes,
the fields of men and women wait
  the sowing of his word.

He will not reap the harvest crop;
  for he will fail and die.
Others must come to reap his work,
  gather his people home.

Jesus, Messiah of God above,
  Jesus, Son of the Father,
sow your words within our hearts
  to grow in love for him.

And raise us up to work with you
  as reapers of the crop
you sowed in the world's widest fields,
  the crop of humankind.

Jesus, let us work with you
  to bring your harvest home!

This Is Truly the Savior of the World

Jn 4:39-45: *Many Samaritans from that city believed in him because of the woman's testimony, "He told me everything I have ever done." So when the Samaritans came to him, they asked him to stay with them; and he stayed there two days. And many more believed because of his word. They said to the woman, "It is no longer because of what you said that we believe, for we have heard for ourselves, and we know that this is truly the Savior of the world."*

When the two days were over, he went from that place to Galilee (for Jesus himself had testified that a prophet has no honor in the prophet's own country). When he came to Galilee, the Galileans welcomed him, since they had seen all that he had done in Jerusalem at the festival; for they too had gone to the festival.

To contemplate:

The simple response
     to Jesus' word:
straightforward faith!
     His word is truth,
utterly transparent.

Yes, testimony
     prepares the way
to firm belief.
     But Jesus' word
is sufficient in itself.

The simple response
     to Jesus' acts:
straightforward faith!
     His acts complete
God's own creative act.

O Jesus, Word
     of God most high,
I do believe in you.

O Jesus, Act
     of your Father-God,
I do believe in you.

O Father, God
     of heaven and earth,
thank you for your Son!

The Reward of Faith

Jn 4:46-54: *Then he came again to Cana in Galilee where he had changed the water into wine. Now there was a royal official whose son lay ill in Capernaum. When he heard that Jesus had come from Judea to Galilee, he went and begged him to come down and heal his son, for he was at the point of death. Then Jesus said to him, "Unless you see signs and wonders you will not believe." The official said to him, "Sir, come down before my little boy dies." Jesus said to him, "Go; your son will live." The man believed the word that Jesus spoke to him and started on his way. As he was going down, his slaves met him and told him that his child was alive. So he asked them the hour when he began to recover, and they said to him, "Yesterday at one in the afternoon the fever left him." The father realized that this was the hour when Jesus had said to him, "Your son will live." So he himself believed, along with his whole household. Now this was the second sign that Jesus did after coming from Judea to Galilee.*

To contemplate:

This father persuades the Son of God
   to heal a little boy.
The man proves his faith by repeated pleas
   for healing of his son.

When Jesus says the boy will live,
   the father believes in Jesus' word—
believes with the heart of a father true,
   who loves his infant son.

True to his word, the Word of God
   worked the cure he pledged:
at the very hour that Jesus spoke,
   the fever left the boy.

This second sign that Jesus worked
   is not unlike the first.
The first rewarded Mary's faith,
   the second, this father's faith.

Like Mary, he believed in Jesus,
   believed his powerful word.
The Word of God makes all anew,
   even the wine of life.

O Jesus, I believe in you;
   I believe your word and act;
for you are the very Word of God,
   and Savior of the world!

Jesus, Equal to God

Jn 5:1-18: *After this there was a festival of the Jews, and Jesus went up to Jerusalem. Now in Jerusalem by the Sheep Gate there is a pool,..which has five porticoes. In these lay many invalids—blind, lame, and paralyzed. One man was there who had been ill for thirty-eight years. When Jesus saw him lying there and knew that he had been there a long time, he said to him, "Do you want to be made well?" The sick man answered him, "Sir, I have no one to put me into the pool when the water is stirred up; and while I am making my way, someone else steps down ahead of me." Jesus said to him, "Stand up, take your mat and walk." At once the man was made well, and he took up his mat and began to walk.*

Now that day was a sabbath. So the Jews said to the man who had been cured, "It is the sabbath; it is not lawful for you to carry your mat." But he answered them, "The man who made me well said to me, 'Take up your mat and walk.'" They asked him, "Who is the man who said to you, 'Take it up and walk'?" Now the man who had been healed did not know who it was, for Jesus had disappeared in the crowd that was there. Later Jesus found him in the temple and said to him, "See, you have been made well! Do not sin any more, so that nothing worse happens to you." The man went away and told

*the Jews that it was Jesus who had made him well.
Therefore the Jews started persecuting Jesus, because he
was doing such things on the sabbath. But Jesus answered them, "My Father is still working, and I also am
working." For this reason the Jews were seeking all the
more to kill him, because he was not only breaking the
sabbath, but was also calling God his own Father,
thereby making himself equal to God.*

To contemplate:

A man, who for thirty-eight years
   has suffered great affliction,
      Jesus heals on the sabbath day!
What makes these religious leaders
   so angry with this healer
      that they desire to kill him?
He has the bold effrontery
   to cure people on the sabbath,
      and call their God his Father!
The leaders tell the healed man that
   he must disobey his healer—
      forget about his cure.
This healer says God always works;
   so he works along with him
      to heal our human ills.
O Jesus, I believe your work
   upholds your word as true—
      I believe you, Son of God,
         equal to your Father!

Who Believes My Word
Has Eternal Life

Jn 5:19-29: *Jesus said to them, "Very truly, I tell you, the Son can do nothing on his own, but only what he sees the Father doing; for whatever the Father does, the Son does likewise. The Father loves the Son and shows him all that he himself is doing; and he will show him greater works than these, so that you will be astonished. Indeed, just as the Father raises the dead and gives them life, so also the Son gives life to whomever he wishes. The Father judges no one but has given all judgment to the Son, so that all may honor the Son just as they honor the Father. Anyone who does not honor the Son does not honor the Father who sent him. Very truly, I tell you, anyone who hears my word and believes him who sent me has eternal life, and does not come under judgment, but has passed from death to life.*

"Very truly, I tell you, the hour is coming, and is now here, when the dead will hear the voice of the Son of God, and those who hear will live. For just as the Father has life in himself, so he has granted the Son also to have life in himself; and he has given him authority to execute judgment, because he is the Son of Man. Do not be astonished at this; for the hour is coming when all who are in their graves will hear his voice and will come out—those who

*have done good, to the resurrection of life, and those who
have done evil, to the resurrection of condemnation."*

To contemplate:

O, how the Father loves his Son,
     and through him all of us!
For he will send the Son of Man
     to judge us men and women!

Since Jesus is the Son of Man,
     he knows us from within;
because he is the Son of God,
     he can raise us up to life.

The test that wins eternal life
     is not a test of will;
the test to win eternal life
     is not a test of mind—
it is a test of simple faith:
     "Do you believe the Son of Man
is also the Son of God,
     equal to his Father?"

O Father, I really do believe
     Jesus is your Son
come as Son of Man for us
     to bring us back to life—
eternal life with you and him,
     resurrection from the dead!

Three Witnesses to Jesus

Jn 5:30-47: *"I can do nothing on my own....*

"If I testify about myself, my testimony is not true. There is another who testifies on my behalf, and I know that his testimony to me is true. You sent messengers to John, and he testified to the truth. Not that I accept such human testimony, but I say these things so that you may be saved. He was a burning and shining lamp, and you were willing to rejoice for a while in his light. But I have a testimony greater than John's. The works that the Father has given me to complete, the very works that I am doing, testify on my behalf that the Father has sent me. And the Father who sent me has himself testified on my behalf. You have never heard his voice or seen his form, and you do not have his word abiding in you, because you do not believe him whom he has sent.

"You search the scriptures because you think that in them you have eternal life; and it is they that testify on my behalf. Yet you refuse to come to me to have life. I do not accept glory from human beings. But I know that you do not have the love of God in you. I have come in my Father's name, and you do not accept me; if another comes in his own name, you will accept him. How can you believe when you accept glory from one another and

do not seek the glory that comes from the one who alone is God? Do not think that I will accuse you before the Father; your accuser is Moses, on whom you have set your hope. If you believed Moses, you would believe me, for he wrote about me. But if you do not believe what he wrote, how will you believe what I say?"

To contemplate:

Three witnesses testify
    to Jesus as Son of God
who came as Son of Man for us—
    three credible witnesses:
"First there was John the Baptist,
    a burning, shining lamp
who testified on my behalf,
    as a light in the wilderness.
Then there were my own works of power:
    changing water into wine,
healing the official's little son
    and the man so long fallen ill.
Finally, the scriptures testify
    to my identity:
Moses foretold that I would come,
    a prophet like himself" (Deut 18:15).

O Jesus, Word and Act of God,
    I do believe in you!
I believe John's heraldic word of you
    and Moses' prophecy.

Jesus Feeds His People

Jn 6:1-15: *After this Jesus went to the other side of the Sea of Galilee, also called the Sea of Tiberias.... When he looked up and saw a large crowd coming toward him, Jesus said to Philip, "Where are we to buy bread for these people to eat?" He said this to test him, for he himself knew what he was going to do. Philip answered him, "Six months' wages would not buy enough bread for each of them to get a little." One of his disciples, Andrew, Simon Peter's brother, said to him, "There is a boy here who has five barley loaves and two fish. But what are they among so many people?" Jesus said, "Make the people sit down." Now there was a great deal of grass in the place; so they sat down, about five thousand in all. Then Jesus took the loaves, and when he had given thanks, he distributed them to those who were seated; so also the fish, as much as they wanted. When they were satisfied, he told his disciples, "Gather up the fragments left over, so that nothing may be lost." So they gathered them up, and from the fragments of the five barley loaves, left by those who had eaten, they filled twelve baskets. When the people saw the sign that he had done, they began to say, "This is indeed the prophet who is to come into the world."*

When Jesus realized that they were about to come and take him by force to make him king, he withdrew again to the mountain by himself.

To contemplate:

As the Passover feast comes near once more,
    Jesus prepares his own new feast
        with another wondrous work:
from five barley loaves and two small fish
    he fills baskets with simple fare
    on which his disciples feed the crowd
        of five thousand hungry folk.
We watch the disciples give out this food
    from baskets that never empty.
And when the thousands have had their fill
    on five loaves of bread and two small fish,
        twelve baskets are left for us.
His providence for his hungry people
    more than satisfies their need.
    They grasp not his love for them,
        but want him for their king.
Today he does much more for us,
    gives us his own flesh for food
        and his blood for drink.
    O Jesus, more than a prophet,
        and more than any king:
    You are our very food and drink—
        our Eucharistic feast!

It Is I; Do Not Be Afraid

Jn 6:16-21: When evening came, his disciples went down to the sea, got into a boat, and started across the sea to Capernaum. It was dark, and Jesus had not yet come to them. The sea became rough because a strong wind was blowing. When they had rowed about three or four miles, they saw Jesus walking on the sea and coming near the boat, and they were terrified. But he said to them, "It is I; do not be afraid." Then they wanted to take him into the boat, and immediately the boat reached the land toward which they were going.

To contemplate:

Jesus' disciples are tossed about
   in their boat upon the waves,
reflecting their Master's dangerous course,
   confronting his opponents.

He has just fed the hungry crowd
   that followed him far from towns;
now he must save his faithful band
   from wind and roaring seas.

It grows dark as pitch as the wind blows up
    and the waves wash over the boat.
They struggle to man the creaking oars
    and bail rising water out.

These hardy, experienced fishermen
    fight for their very lives;
they know they have but little time
    to survive the howling sea.

And then when their efforts seem in vain,
    there appears a strange lone form.
Only a ghost could walk these waves—
    it must be the ghost of Death!

But no, it is not Death himself
    who comes striding on the waves—
it is the very Lord of Life,
    who saves his fishermen!

Like Yahweh of old Jesus walks the sea (Ps 77:19)
    to protect his own from death.

O Jesus, stride over my waves of stress;
    tell me, "It is I, fear not!"

The Bread of God Gives Life

Jn 6:22-34: *The next day the crowd that had stayed on the other side of the sea saw that there had been only one boat there. They also saw that Jesus had not got into the boat with his disciples, but that his disciples had gone away alone. Then some boats from Tiberias came near the place where they had eaten the bread after the Lord had given thanks. So when the crowd saw that neither Jesus nor his disciples were there, they themselves got into the boats and went to Capernaum looking for Jesus.*

When they found him on the other side of the sea, they said to him, "Rabbi, when did you come here?" Jesus answered them, "Very truly, I tell you, you are looking for me, not because you saw signs, but because you ate your fill of the loaves. Do not work for the food that perishes, but for the food that endures for eternal life, which the Son of Man will give you. For it is on him that God the Father has set his seal." Then they said to him, "What must we do to perform the works of God?" Jesus answered them, "This is the work of God, that you believe in him whom he has sent." So they said to him, "What sign are you going to give us then, so that we may see it and believe you? What work are you performing? Our ancestors ate the manna in the wilderness; as

it is written, 'He gave them bread from heaven to eat.'"
Then Jesus said to them, "Very truly, I tell you, it was
not Moses who gave you the bread from heaven, but it is
my Father who gives you the true bread from heaven.
For the bread of God is that which comes down from
heaven and gives life to the world." They said to him,
"Sir, give us this bread always."

To contemplate:

There is a more important food
   than that we daily eat;
it is, indeed, worth asking for,
   this food of the Son of Man.

For it is a food beyond our reach,
   a food beyond our merit;
only the Son of Man himself
   can give us food from heaven.

He sets a condition for this food:
   to believe he has been sent
by the Father above who gave the manna
   that Moses asked him for.

Greater than manna is this new bread;
   it is true *bread of heaven!*
It is the bread of God himself
   bringing life to our broken world.

They ask him at once to give this bread.
   We, too, beg for it, Lord!

I Am the Bread of Life

Jn 6:35-50: *Jesus said to them, "I am the bread of life. Whoever comes to me will never be hungry, and whoever believes in me will never be thirsty. But I said to you that you have seen me and yet do not believe. Everything that the Father gives me will come to me, and anyone who comes to me I will never drive away; for I have come down from heaven, not to do my own will, but the will of him who sent me. And this is the will of him who sent me, that I should lose nothing of all that he has given me, but raise it up on the last day. This is indeed the will of my Father, that all who see the Son and believe in him may have eternal life; and I will raise them up on the last day."*

Then the Jews began to complain about him because he said, "I am the bread that came down from heaven." They were saying, "Is not this Jesus, the son of Joseph, whose father and mother we know? How can he now say, 'I have come down from heaven'?" Jesus answered them, "Do not complain among yourselves. No one can come to me unless drawn by the Father who sent me; and I will raise that person up on the last day. It is written in the prophets, 'And they shall all be taught by God.' Everyone who has heard and learned from the Father comes to me. Not that anyone has seen the Father except the one who is from God; he has seen the Father. Very truly, I tell you, whoever believes has eternal life. I am the bread of life. Your ancestors ate the manna in the wilderness, and they died. This is the bread that comes down from heaven, so that one may eat of it and not die."

To contemplate:

They think they know his origin
   within the human race;
they won't believe he comes from heaven
   to give himself to them.

Do we refuse to believe in him
   as our true bread from heaven?
Do we refuse our love for him
   who gives himself to us?

Bread is the staple of body life;
   Jesus, staple of spirit life!
We hunger for our daily bread.
   Do we hunger for our Lord?

When Israel asked for desert food,
   God gave manna from above.
When we languish in our secular world,
   Jesus offers himself to us.

O Jesus, give me faith in you!

O Jesus, be my bread of life!

Eat My Flesh and Drink My Blood

Jn 6:51-59: *"I am the living bread that came down from heaven. Whoever eats of this bread will live forever; and the bread that I will give for the life of the world is my flesh."*

The Jews then disputed among themselves, saying, "How can this man give us his flesh to eat?" So Jesus said to them, "Very truly, I tell you, unless you eat the flesh of the Son of Man and drink his blood, you have no life in you. Those who eat my flesh and drink my blood have eternal life, and I will raise them up on the last day; for my flesh is true food and my blood is true drink. Those who eat my flesh and drink my blood abide in me, and I in them. Just as the living Father sent me, and I live because of the Father, so whoever eats me will live because of me. This is the bread that came down from heaven, not like that which your ancestors ate, and they died. But the one who eats this bread will live forever." He said these things while he was teaching in the synagogue at Capernaum.

To contemplate:

Suddenly he speaks in literal terms—
    "bread of life" is more than sign,
built upon our daily bread,
    or manna in Sinai's desert.
"Bread of life" is "flesh to eat";
    "blood of life" is "blood to drink."
Jesus is truly flesh and blood—
    flesh to eat, blood to drink.

Can he expect the people
    to accept this awesome word?
And when they stagger in disbelief,
    can he still insist on faith?
He plunges on: "*Unless* you eat,
    eat my flesh and drink my blood,
you have no true life in you!"
    How can we *eat you*, Lord?

O bewildering word that sent away
    nearly all your followers.
O mystery that staggers faith
    all down historic years.

O Jesus, open my mind and heart
    to your mysterious truth:
I believe you give your flesh to eat
    and your very blood to drink!

If we believe you "became our flesh,"
why not "I give you my flesh to eat"?

You Have the Words of Eternal Life

Jn 6:60-71: *When many of his disciples heard it, they said, "This teaching is difficult; who can accept it?" But Jesus, being aware that his disciples were complaining about it, said to them, "Does this offend you? Then what if you were to see the Son of Man ascending to where he was before? It is the spirit that gives life; the flesh is useless. The words that I have spoken to you are spirit and life. But among you there are some who do not believe." For Jesus knew from the first who were the ones that did not believe, and who was the one that would betray him. And he said, "For this reason I have told you that no one can come to me unless it is granted by the Father."*

Because of this many of his disciples turned back and no longer went about with him. So Jesus asked the twelve, "Do you also wish to go away?" Simon Peter answered him, "Lord, to whom can we go? You have the words of eternal life. We have come to believe and know that you are the Holy One of God." Jesus answered them, "Did I not choose you, the twelve? Yet one of you is a devil." He was speaking of Judas son of Simon Iscariot, for he, though one of the twelve, was going to betray him.

To contemplate:

They begin to walk away from him;
   he does not call them back
to explain away what he has said:
   "I'll give you my flesh to eat!"

Instead, he hurls a further test:
   "And what if you should see
the Son of Man ascend to heaven,
   the place from which he came?

"The words I spoke, though literal,
   are words of spirit and life.
Look far below their surface sense
   to find their deeper meaning."

Though Peter does not grasp your word,
   he believes *you are the Word:*
"You have the words of eternal life;
   we grasp not, yet believe!"

Then another shocking revelation:
   "Is not one of you a devil?"
Jesus, do you reveal your gift
   even to your betrayer?

Will you offer your flesh and blood
   even to Judas—to save us?

The World's Unbelief

Jn 7:1-13: *After this Jesus went about in Galilee. He did not wish to go about in Judea because the Jews were looking for an opportunity to kill him. Now the Jewish festival of Booths was near. So his brothers said to him, "Leave here and go to Judea so that your disciples also may see the works you are doing; for no one who wants to be widely known acts in secret. If you do these things, show yourself to the world." (For not even his brothers believed in him.) Jesus said to them, "My time has not yet come, but your time is always here. The world cannot hate you, but it hates me because I testify against it that its works are evil. Go to the festival yourselves. I am not going to this festival, for my time has not yet fully come." After saying this, he remained in Galilee.*

But after his brothers had gone to the festival, then he also went, not publicly but as it were in secret. The Jews were looking for him at the festival and saying, "Where is he?" And there was considerable complaining about him among the crowds. While some were saying, "He is a good man," others were saying, "No, he is deceiving the crowd." Yet no one would speak openly about him for fear of the Jews.

To contemplate:

Jesus testifies the world hates him,
    not because he does it harm,
    not because he deceives the crowd,
but because he uncovers its evil ways.

His relatives think he craves its praise
    for his healing of the ill
    and his preaching of his word;
his relatives do not believe in him.

He knows his time has not yet come;
    if the world knows he'll go,
    some will even plot his death;
so he must go clandestinely.

The crowd is divided over him:
    some praise him as truly good;
    others condemn him as bad.
But all fear to speak openly of him.

Jesus, is it not the same today?
    Some want to follow you;
    others despise your name—
to many you're a topic unpopular.

Jesus, loosen my self-conscious tongue
    to speak fearlessly for you!

Do Not Judge by Appearances

Jn 7:14-24: *About the middle of the festival Jesus went up into the temple and began to teach. The Jews were astonished at it, saying, "How does this man have such learning, when he has never been taught?" Then Jesus answered them, "My teaching is not mine but his who sent me. Anyone who resolves to do the will of God will know whether the teaching is from God or whether I am speaking on my own. Those who speak on their own seek their own glory; but the one who seeks the glory of him who sent him is true, and there is nothing false in him.*

"Did not Moses give you the law? Yet none of you keeps the law. Why are you looking for an opportunity to kill me?" The crowd answered, "You have a demon! Who is trying to kill you?" Jesus answered them, "I performed one work, and all of you are astonished. Moses gave you circumcision (it is, of course, not from Moses, but from the patriarchs), and you circumcise a man on the sabbath. If a man receives circumcision on the sabbath in order that the law of Moses may not be broken, are you angry with me because I healed a man's whole body on the sabbath? Do not judge by appearances, but judge with right judgment."

To contemplate:

"My teaching is not mine alone;
     it is his who sent me to you."
God's Son is a truly humble man;
     he seeks not his own will,
     only his Father's will.

Jesus is not rabbi-taught;
     neither is he self-taught.
Jesus is only Father-taught!
     Those who seek God's will
     know Jesus teaches truth.

With impassioned, angry words
     he reveals another truth:
they seek to take his life!
     They wrongfully deny—
     they deny the truth.

Do I seek the harm of those
     who speak to me the truth?
Does prejudice make me blind?
     Or with honest heart
     can I acknowledge where truth lies?

O fearless Lord, let me be one
     who stands with you for truth—
     and does not judge by appearances!

You Know Where I Am From

Jn 7:25-36: *Now some of the people of Jerusalem were saying, "Is not this the man whom they are trying to kill? And here he is, speaking openly, but they say nothing to him! Can it be that the authorities really know that this is the Messiah? Yet we know where this man is from; but when the Messiah comes, no one will know where he is from." Then Jesus cried out as he was teaching in the temple, "You know me, and you know where I am from. I have not come on my own. But the one who sent me is true, and you do not know him. I know him, because I am from him, and he sent me." Then they tried to arrest him, but no one laid hands on him, because his hour had not yet come. Yet many in the crowd believed in him and were saying, "When the Messiah comes, will he do more signs than this man has done?"*

The Pharisees heard the crowd muttering such things about him, and the chief priests and Pharisees sent temple police to arrest him. Jesus then said, "I will be with you a little while longer, and then I am going to him who sent me. You will search for me, but you will not find me; and where I am, you cannot come." The Jews said to one another, "Where does this man intend to go that we will not find him? Does he intend to go to

*the Dispersion among the Greeks and teach the Greeks?
What does he mean by saying, 'You will search for me
and you will not find me' and 'Where I am, you cannot
come'?"*

To contemplate:

They think they know his origin—
 from Nazareth, of course.
But he is from his Father above—
 our Father who is in heaven.

If only they would listen to him,
 they could know this great truth.
But most do not hear his word;
 they listen to another call.

The Pharisees are listening, though,
 listening to the wavering crowd.
They send police to capture him,
 but he is in control—
 his time has not yet come.

He promises he'll soon be gone—
 gone to him from whom he's come.
They will search for him in vain;
 they cannot climb to heaven.

O Jesus, I would search for you,
 find you in your Father's presence.
O Jesus, I know where you are—
 bring me to your Father's house!

You Who Are Thirsty, Come to Me

Jn 7:37-52: *On the last day of the festival, the great day, while Jesus was standing there, he cried out, "Let anyone who is thirsty come to me, and let the one who believes in me drink. As the scripture has said, 'Out of the believer's heart shall flow rivers of living water.'" Now he said this about the Spirit, which believers in him were to receive; for as yet there was no Spirit, because Jesus was not yet glorified.*

When they heard these words, some in the crowd said, "This is really the prophet." Others said, "This is the Messiah." But some asked, "Surely the Messiah does not come from Galilee, does he? Has not the scripture said that the Messiah is descended from David and comes from Bethlehem, the village where David lived?" So there was a division in the crowd because of him. Some of them wanted to arrest him, but no one laid hands on him.

Then the temple police went back to the chief priests and Pharisees, who asked them, "Why did you not arrest him?" The police answered, "Never has anyone spoken like this!" Then the Pharisees replied, "Surely you have not been deceived too, have you? Has any one of the authorities or of the Pharisees believed in him? But this

*crowd, which does not know the law—they are ac-
cursed." Nicodemus, who had gone to Jesus before, and
who was one of them, asked, "Our law does not judge
people without first giving them a hearing to find out
what they are doing, does it?" They replied, "Surely you
are not also from Galilee, are you? Search and you will
see that no prophet is to arise from Galilee."*

To contemplate:

Jeremiah had called the Lord our God
   "the fountain of living water" (Jer 17:13),
symbolized by harvest rain
   poured out upon the altar
   of God's most holy temple.
Jesus told the Samaritan woman
   he could give her living water;
now he reveals himself as Lord,
   sender of this living water:
   his own refreshing Spirit.
So strong is Jesus' claim as Lord,
   even temple police are moved:
"Never did anyone speak like this!"
   But others angrily object:
   "No prophet comes from Galilee."
O Jesus, you'll be killed for this claim—
   this claim to be the Lord.
Nicodemus cannot save you now—
   you speak too recklessly.
   Yet I believe your claim!

Go Your Way and Do Not Sin Again

Jn 8:1-11: *Then each of them went home, while Jesus went to the Mount of Olives. Early in the morning he came again to the temple. All the people came to him and he sat down and began to teach them. The scribes and the Pharisees brought a woman who had been caught in adultery; and making her stand before all of them, they said to him, "Teacher, this woman was caught in the very act of committing adultery. Now in the law Moses commanded us to stone such women. Now what do you say?" They said this to test him, so that they might have some charge to bring against him. Jesus bent down and wrote with his finger on the ground. When they kept on questioning him, he straightened up and said to them, "Let anyone among you who is without sin be the first to throw a stone at her." And once again he bent down and wrote on the ground. When they heard it, they went away, one by one, beginning with the elders; and Jesus was left alone with the woman standing before him. Jesus straightened up and said to her, "Woman, where are they? Has no one condemned you?" She said, "No one, sir." And Jesus said, "Neither do I condemn you. Go your way, and from now on do not sin again."*

To contemplate:

What is Jesus writing upon the ground—
the names of those ready to throw the stones?

Jeremiah had written many centuries before:
"All who forsake you, Lord, shall be put to shame,
and their names recorded in the underworld;
they have forsaken the fountain of living water"
(Jer 17:13).

All the would-be stoners are found with sin—
they slink away in shame to see their names
written in the dust of the underworld,
written by the Lord who sees their hearts.

Yet Jesus is gentle with the adulteress;
her sin was one of weakness, not of pride.
He does not condone her sin, yet he forgives:
"Go on your way and do not sin again."

Lord, you reveal a justice-giving God
who writes the names of tyrants in the dust;
yet yours is also a tender-hearted God
who saves the oppressed from tyranny
and forgives their sins of weakness with a word
of gentle reproof and kind encouragement.

O Jesus, Lord of living, saving water,
Lord of harvest rain and harvest crop,
    be my own sweet Lord of kindly heart!

I Am the Light of the World

Jn 8:12-20: *Again Jesus spoke to them, saying, "I am the light of the world. Whoever follows me will never walk in darkness but will have the light of life." Then the Pharisees said to him, "You are testifying on your own behalf; your testimony is not valid." Jesus answered, "Even if I testify on my own behalf, my testimony is valid because I know where I have come from and where I am going, but you do not know where I come from or where I am going. You judge by human standards; I judge no one. Yet even if I do judge, my judgment is valid; for it is not I alone who judge, but I and the Father who sent me. In your law it is written that the testimony of two witnesses is valid. I testify on my own behalf, and the Father who sent me testifies on my behalf." Then they said to him, "Where is your Father?" Jesus answered, "You know neither me nor my Father. If you knew me, you would know my Father also." He spoke these words while he was teaching in the treasury of the temple, but no one arrested him, because his hour had not yet come.*

To contemplate:

God made all things through his Word,
    the Word that is his Wisdom.
The first thing his Word made was light,
    for his Word is light itself—
not the outer light of our poor world,
    but the inner light of spirit.

Then the light entered the world,
    so we might not walk in darkness—
he taught about God and his great love,
    as the prophets had taught the people.
But Jesus went even deeper
    to show us God's heart as the Son.

So now at last the light shines forth;
    yet some people failed to see.
They quibbled about the source of light
    and missed the light himself,
even though the source of light
    bore witness in Jesus' signs.

May I know the Father and the Son,
    know both the light and its source,
may I seek to dwell in the light of God,
    to know his truth and his love.

O Jesus, light of all the world,
    light up my way to life!

I Always Do
What Is Pleasing to Him

Jn 8:21-30: *Again he said to them, "I am going away, and you will search for me, but you will die in your sin. Where I am going, you cannot come." Then the Jews said, "Is he going to kill himself? Is that what he means by saying, 'Where I am going, you cannot come'?" He said to them, "You are from below, I am from above; you are of this world, I am not of this world. I told you that you would die in your sins, for you will die in your sins unless you believe that I am he." They said to him, "Who are you?" Jesus said to them, "Why do I speak to you at all? I have much to say about you and much to condemn; but the one who sent me is true, and I declare to the world what I have heard from him." They did not understand that he was speaking to them about the Father. So Jesus said, "When you have lifted up the Son of Man, then you will realize that I am he, and that I do nothing on my own, but I speak these things as the Father instructed me. And the one who sent me is with me; he has not left me alone, for I always do what is pleasing to him." As he was saying these things, many believed in him.*

To contemplate:

"The one who sent me is still with me;
  he has not left me alone.
I always do what is pleasing to him,
  for I know his will for us."

What pleases God—that is our call,
  our key to happiness.
And only the one who comes from God
  knows his will for us.

Only the one who works with God
  knows the nature he gave to us.
Only the one who comes from God
  bears his light for us.

O Jesus, because you come from God,
  we listen to your word;
for you yourself are his very Word
  and light from his own light.

We know you because you were "lifted up,"
  high upon Calvary's cross.
We know your love must be divine—
  only you have died for us.

O Jesus, we stand with those who hear
  and believe you love as God;
O Jesus, you show how God loves us—
  enough to die for us!

The Truth Will Make You Free

Jn 8:31-38: *Then Jesus said to the Jews who had believed in him, "If you continue in my word, you are truly my disciples; and you will know the truth, and the truth will make you free." They answered him, "We are descendants of Abraham and have never been slaves to anyone. What do you mean by saying, 'You will be made free'?"*

Jesus answered them, "Very truly, I tell you, everyone who commits sin is a slave to sin. The slave does not have a permanent place in the household; the son has a place there forever. So if the Son makes you free, you will be free indeed. I know that you are descendants of Abraham; yet you look for an opportunity to kill me, because there is no place in you for my word. I declare what I have seen in the Father's presence; as for you, you should do what you have heard from the Father."

To contemplate:

The lie ties up our minds in chains;
   the lie binds up our hearts.
The abortion lie, euthanasia lie,
   are killing society.

If we can lie about life and death,
    we can lie about anything.
Then, indeed, do we make ourselves
    slaves to every sin.

Only the truth can set us free,
    free our minds from dishonesty,
free our hearts from perversity,
    free our selves from selfishness.

Only the truth about our God,
    and the truth about ourselves,
only the truth about the world—
    the truth can set us free.

And only the light can show us truth,
    only the Lord of Light:
"Would you be slave or would you be free?
    Choose for eternity!"

O Jesus, light of our very life,
    I choose to follow you.
O Jesus, chosen Son of Man,
    you see within our hearts.
O Jesus, Son of God himself,
    make us free at last!

Whoever Is from God
Hears the Words of God

Jn 8:39-47: *They answered him, "Abraham is our father." Jesus said to them, "If you were Abraham's children, you would be doing what Abraham did, but now you are trying to kill me, a man who has told you the truth that I heard from God. This is not what Abraham did. You are indeed doing what your father does." They said to him, "We are not illegitimate children; we have one father, God himself." Jesus said to them, "If God were your Father, you would love me, for I came from God and now I am here. I did not come on my own, but he sent me. Why do you not understand what I say? It is because you cannot accept my word. You are from your father the devil, and you choose to do your father's desires. He was a murderer from the beginning and does not stand in the truth, because there is no truth in him. When he lies, he speaks according to his own nature, for he is a liar and the father of lies. But because I tell the truth, you do not believe me. Which of you convicts me of sin? If I tell the truth, why do you not believe me? Whoever is from God hears the words of God. The reason you do not hear them is that you are not from God."*

To contemplate:

God chose Abraham as our father in faith.
　　Do I act as his true heir?
I claim God himself for my Father,
　　how well do I really know him?

Jesus says: "God is the Father that I know,
　　the Father who taught me truth,
the Father whom I reveal to you—
　　the Father who is all-Good."

O Jesus, you look into our hearts
　　and see whose children we are!
Do my actions show to others
　　that I'm a child of your Father-God?

O Son of Man and Son of God,
　　help me be like you!

Before Abraham Was, I AM

Jn 8:48-59: *The Jews answered him, "Are we not right i1 saying that you are a Samaritan and have a demon?" Jesus answered, "I do not have a demon; but I honor my Father, and you dishonor me. Yet I do not seek my own glory; there is one who seeks it and he is the judge. Very truly, I tell you, whoever keeps my word will never see death." The Jews said to him, "Now we know that you have a demon. Abraham died, and so did the prophets; yet you say, 'Whoever keeps my word will never taste death.' Are you greater than our father Abraham, who died? The prophets also died. Who do you claim to be?" Jesus answered, "If I glorify myself, my glory is nothing. It is my Father who glorifies me, he of whom you say, 'He is our God,' though you do not know him. But I know him; if I would say that I do not know him, I would be a liar like you. But I do know him and I keep his word. Your ancestor Abraham rejoiced that he would see my day; he saw it and was glad." Then the Jews said to him, "You are not yet fifty years old, and have you seen Abraham?" Jesus said to them, "Very truly, I tell you, before Abraham was, I am." So they picked up stones to throw at him, but Jesus hid himself and went out of the temple.*

To contemplate:

At the burning bush Moses knelt
　　and asked of God his name;
and God replied, "I AM WHO AM—
　　my true name is 'I AM'!"

And so when the Jews now ask of Jesus,
　　"Who do you claim to be?"
it is more than a simple question
　　that they are asking him;

and his is more than a simple answer:
　　"Before Abraham was, I AM."
Their minds go back to the burning bush—
　　he claims to be *Yahweh!*

What man could utter such a claim—
　　it staggers the Jewish mind.
It still staggers the Christian mind.
　　Who is this Jesus Christ?

A madman or blaspheming liar—
　　there is no in-between.
Yet could his claim be really true?
　　Consider his words and works!

O Jesus, neither mad nor false,
　　"You are my Lord and God!"

I Am the Light of the World

Jn 9:1-12: *As he walked along, he saw a man blind from birth. His disciples asked him, "Rabbi, who sinned, this man or his parents, that he was born blind?" Jesus answered, "Neither this man nor his parents sinned; he was born blind so that God's works might be revealed in him. We must work the works of him who sent me while it is day; night is coming when no one can work. As long as I am in the world, I am the light of the world." When he had said this, he spat on the ground and made mud with the saliva and spread the mud on the man's eyes, saying to him, "Go, wash in the pool of Siloam" (which means Sent). Then he went and washed and came back able to see. The neighbors and those who had seen him before as a beggar began to ask, "Is this not the man who used to sit and beg?" Some were saying, "It is he." Others were saying, "No, but it is someone like him." He kept saying, "I am the man." But they kept asking him, "Then how were your eyes opened?" He answered, "The man called Jesus made mud, spread it on my eyes, and said to me, 'Go to Siloam and wash.' Then I went and washed and received my sight." They said to him, "Where is he?" He said, "I do not know."*

To contemplate:

The man who claims to be the light
　　now offers solid proof:
he gives new sight to a beggar man
　　who has never seen the light.

After the way of the God of old
　　who made us from the earth,
with a little mud Jesus rubs his eyes
　　to make them see at last.

This is not just a simple cure
　　like healing ailing eyes;
this is a true creative act
　　of making something new.

So some in the crowd will not believe
　　that this is the beggar man
who was blind from his mother's womb;
　　but others do not doubt.

He recites the simple recipe
　　of how the act was done.
They want to see the man again
　　who works with such great might.

Dear Lord, you loved the beggar man.
　　Be light for my inner sight!

How Can a Sinner
Perform Such Signs?

Jn 9:13-23: *They brought to the Pharisees the man who had formerly been blind. Now it was a sabbath day when Jesus made the mud and opened his eyes. Then the Pharisees also began to ask him how he had received his sight. He said to them, "He put mud on my eyes. Then I washed, and now I see." Some of the Pharisees said, "This man is not from God, for he does not observe the sabbath." But others said, "How can a man who is a sinner perform such signs?" And they were divided. So they said again to the blind man, "What do you say about him? It was your eyes he opened." He said, "He is a prophet."*

The Jews did not believe that he had been blind and had received his sight until they called the parents of the man who had received his sight and asked them, "Is this your son, who you say was born blind? How then does he now see?" His parents answered, "We know that this is our son, and that he was born blind; but we do not know how it is that now he sees, nor do we know who opened his eyes. Ask him; he is of age. He will speak for himself." His parents said this because they were afraid of the Jews; for the Jews had already agreed that anyone who confessed Jesus to be the Messiah would be put out of the synagogue. Therefore his parents said, "He is of age; ask him."

To contemplate:

The proof is there before their eyes,
    in the eyes of the man born blind;
yet some cling for life to their unbelief
    instead of to the Lord!

And are we not like that today,
    when we cling for life to things
of little or no real consequence,
    instead of the God of life?

Are we not like that if we accept
    the lie that life is death:
the lie that anyone has a right
    to kill an unborn child?
Are we not like that if we accept
    the lie that death is life:
the lie that it's right to kill people
    to relieve them of their pain?

O Jesus, God of light and life,
    give us light to see aright!

Now I See!

Jn 9:24-34: *So for the second time they called the man who had been blind, and they said to him, "Give glory to God! We know that this man is a sinner." He answered, "I do not know whether he is a sinner. One thing I do know, that though I was blind, now I see." They said to him, "What did he do to you? How did he open your eyes?" He answered them, "I have told you already, and you would not listen. Why do you want to hear it again? Do you also want to become his disciples?" Then they reviled him, saying, "You are his disciple, but we are disciples of Moses. We know that God has spoken to Moses, but as for this man, we do not know where he comes from." The man answered, "Here is an astonishing thing! You do not know where he comes from, and yet he opened my eyes. We know that God does not listen to sinners, but he does listen to one who worships him and obeys his will. Never since the world began has it been heard that anyone opened the eyes of a person born blind. If this man were not from God, he could do nothing." They answered him, "You were born entirely in sins, and are you trying to teach us?" And they drove him out.*

To contemplate:

"Give glory to God, not to this man,
    for he is only a sinner!"
"I only know one simple thing—
    I was blind and now I see!"

The learned men get nothing right;
    the simple man is wise.
God uses the little ones of this world
    to confuse the self-styled "great."

The teachers squirm and try again
    to twist the beggar's mind,
but the simple man goes to the point:
    "Without God, what could he do?

"Never since God made the world
    has one born blind been cured;
if this healer were not from God,
    could he have given me eyes?"

At last they have nothing left to say,
    but they stand on their dignity;
instead of admitting the beggar's right,
    they drive him from their sight.

O Jesus, Creator of this new light,
    open our inner sight!

Faith in the Son of Man
Is the Test of Sight

Jn 9:35-41: *Jesus heard that they had driven him out, and when he found him, he said, "Do you believe in the Son of Man?" He answered, "And who is he, sir? Tell me, so that I may believe in him." Jesus said to him, "You have seen him, and the one speaking with you is he." He said, "Lord, I believe." And he worshiped him. Jesus said, "I came into this world for judgment so that those who do not see may see, and those who do see may become blind." Some of the Pharisees near him heard this and said to him, "Surely we are not blind, are we?" Jesus said to them, "If you were blind, you would not have sin. But now that you say, 'We see,' your sin remains."*

To contemplate:

The Son of Man is the judge of all;
   he sees into all hearts.
He distinguishes those who seek the truth
   from those who blind themselves.

The blind beggar has kept his mind
    open to see God's truth;
while others have closed their hearts
    to God's pure inner law.

Jesus does not make them blind;
    they have blinded themselves;
he only uncovers their hidden sin
    of closing up their hearts.

Had their blindness not been self-imposed
    they would have no sin;
so when they say they see but don't,
    they commit a greater sin.

O Son of Man and judge of all,
    heal our inner sight;
open up our half-closed minds
    to all your gospel truth.

O Son of God and king of all,
    open our half-closed hearts
to the prompting of your Holy Spirit,
    that we may love your truth.

O Jesus, greater than Abraham,
    we adore you as our God!

I Am the Gate of Salvation

Jn 10:1-10: *"Very truly, I tell you, anyone who does not enter the sheepfold by the gate but climbs in by another way is a thief and a bandit. The one who enters by the gate is the shepherd of the sheep. The gatekeeper opens the gate for him, and the sheep hear his voice. He calls his own sheep by name and leads them out. When he has brought out all his own, he goes ahead of them, and the sheep follow him because they know his voice. They will not follow a stranger, but they will run from him because they do not know the voice of strangers."* Jesus used this figure of speech with them, but they did not understand what he was saying to them.

So again Jesus said to them, *"Very truly, I tell you, I am the gate for the sheep. All who came before me are thieves and bandits; but the sheep did not listen to them. I am the gate. Whoever enters by me will be saved, and will come in and go out and find pasture. The thief comes only to steal and kill and destroy. I came that they may have life, and have it abundantly."*

To contemplate:

The rural people of Jesus' day
    prized their flocks of sheep.
So Jesus uses images,
    derived from the life they know.

First, he portrays his care for them
    as the gate that guards the sheep
from thieves who want to capture them
    and bandits who would kill.

As long as the sheepfold gate is closed,
    the sheep are safe inside.
The gate is opened for only those
    to whom the sheep belong.

After a long day in the sun,
    the gate is a welcome sight;
they enter to be safe at night
    from all that would do them harm.

After our long day in the sun,
    as nightfall threatens us,
we'll find an everlasting haven,
    if we hear Jesus' call.

O Jesus, be my saving gate,
    protect me from the night
relentlessly closing in on me—
    be my abundant life!

I Am the Good Shepherd

Jn 10:11-21: *"I am the good shepherd. The good shepherd lays down his life for the sheep. The hired hand, who is not the shepherd and does not own the sheep, sees the wolf coming and leaves the sheep and runs away—and the wolf snatches them and scatters them. The hired hand runs away because a hired hand does not care for the sheep. I am the good shepherd. I know my own and my own know me, just as the Father knows me and I know the Father. And I lay down my life for the sheep. I have other sheep that do not belong to this fold. I must bring them also, and they will listen to my voice. So there will be one flock, one shepherd. For this reason the Father loves me, because I lay down my life in order to take it up again. No one takes it from me, but I lay it down of my own accord. I have power to lay it down, and I have power to take it up again. I have received this command from my Father."*

Again the Jews were divided because of these words. Many of them were saying, "He has a demon and is out of his mind. Why listen to him?" Others were saying, "These are not the words of one who has a demon. Can a demon open the eyes of the blind?"

To contemplate:

More than the gate to save the sheep,
   Jesus is our shepherd—
not just one hired to do a job,
   but the owner of the sheep.

Other shepherds are hireling guards
   who care not for the sheep.
When the wolf comes to snatch their wards,
   they run away and hide.

But Jesus knows us all by name;
   he knows us in the Father.
As the Father knows him, he knows us—
   most intimately.

When Satan comes to snatch us,
   Jesus will stand his ground,
even mount his cross on Calvary—
   lay down his life for us!

Though God's own Son, he will die for us;
   for he has the power to die—
to give up his life and raise it again,
   and raise us up with him.

O Jesus, Lord of life and death,
   shepherd my poor heart!

The Father and I Are One

Jn 10:22-39: *At that time the festival of the Dedication took place in Jerusalem. It was winter, and Jesus was walking in the temple, in the portico of Solomon. So the Jews gathered around him and said to him, "How long will you keep us in suspense? If you are the Messiah, tell us plainly." Jesus answered, "I have told you, and you do not believe. The works that I do in my Father's name testify to me; but you do not believe, because you do not belong to my sheep. My sheep hear my voice. I know them, and they follow me. I give them eternal life, and they will never perish. No one will snatch them out of my hand. What my Father has given me is greater than all else, and no one can snatch it out of the Father's hand. The Father and I are one."*

The Jews took up stones again to stone him. Jesus replied, "I have shown you many good works from the Father. For which of these are you going to stone me?" The Jews answered, "It is not for a good work that we are going to stone you, but for blasphemy, because you, though only a human being, are making yourself God." Jesus answered, "Is it not written in your law, 'I said, you are gods'? If those to whom the word of God came were called 'gods'—and the scripture cannot be annulled—can you say that the one whom the Father has sanctified and sent into the world is blaspheming because I said, 'I am God's Son'? If I am not doing the works of my Father, then do not believe me. But if I do them, even though you do not believe me, believe the works, so that you may know and understand that the Father is in me and I am in the Father." Then they tried to arrest him again, but he escaped from their hands.

To contemplate:

"You do not believe—you are not my sheep.
   My sheep hear my voice."
O Jesus, I do believe in you—
   I listen to your voice.

"I know them and they follow me.
   I give them eternal life."
O Jesus, I do try to follow you;
   give me eternal life.

"No one will snatch them from my hand—
   the Father gives them to me."
O Father, you've given me to your Son!
   I entrust myself to him.

"The Father and I are one—one God.
   He is in me and I in him."
O Jesus, I believe you are God's Son;
   I revere you as my Lord.

Father, thank you for my good shepherd.
   Jesus, I follow you!

Lord, He Whom You Love Is Ill

Jn 10:40-11:16: He went away again across the Jordan to the place where John had been baptizing earlier, and he remained there. Many came to him, and they were saying, "John performed no sign, but everything that John said about this man was true." And many believed in him there.

Now a certain man was ill, Lazarus of Bethany, the village of Mary and her sister Martha. Mary was the one who anointed the Lord with perfume and wiped his feet with her hair; her brother Lazarus was ill. So the sisters sent a message to Jesus, "Lord, he whom you love is ill." But when Jesus heard it, he said, "This illness does not lead to death; rather it is for God's glory, so that the Son of God may be glorified through it." Accordingly, though Jesus loved Martha and her sister and Lazarus, after having heard that Lazarus was ill, he stayed two days longer in the place where he was. Then after this he said to the disciples, "Let us go to Judea again." The disciples said to him, "Rabbi, the Jews were just now trying to stone you, and are you going there again?" Jesus answered, "Are there not twelve hours of daylight? Those who walk during the day do not stumble, because they see the light of this world. But those who walk at night stumble, because the light is not in them." After saying

this, he told them, "Our friend Lazarus has fallen asleep,
but I am going there to awaken him." The disciples said
to him, "Lord, if he has fallen asleep, he will be all
right." Jesus, however, had been speaking about his
death, but they thought that he was referring merely to
sleep. Then Jesus told them plainly, "Lazarus is dead.
For your sake I am glad I was not there, so that you may
believe. But let us go to him." Thomas, who was called
the Twin, said to his fellow disciples, "Let us also go,
that we may die with him."

To contemplate:

Jesus, one of your sheep is ill—
    why do you tarry here?
Is that the way the good shepherd
    cares for a sheep he loves?

O light of the world, why do you let
    your friend die in the dark?
Lazarus is dying, Lord of life—
    why do you tarry here?

Yet how can you return to him?
    They tried to stone you there.
Thomas the doubter believes in you:
    "Let us go and die with him."

O Jesus, another sheep needs you—
    I, too, sink toward the tomb.
Come to my rescue, my shepherd—
    save me from nothingness!

I Am the Resurrection and the Life!

Jn 11:17-27: *When Jesus arrived, he found that Lazarus had already been in the tomb four days. Now Bethany was near Jerusalem, some two miles away, and many of the Jews had come to Martha and Mary to console them about their brother. When Martha heard that Jesus was coming, she went and met him, while Mary stayed at home. Martha said to Jesus, "Lord, if you had been here, my brother would not have died. But even now I know that God will give you whatever you ask of him." Jesus said to her, "Your brother will rise again." Martha said to him, "I know that he will rise again in the resurrection on the last day." Jesus said to her, "I am the resurrection and the life. Those who believe in me, even though they die, will live, and everyone who lives and believes in me will never die. Do you believe this?" She said to him, "Yes, Lord, I believe that you are the Messiah, the Son of God, the one coming into the world."*

To contemplate:

O Martha, do you really believe
  that Jesus can raise your brother—
raise him back to life again
  out of the blackest tomb?

Like Mary, Jesus' mother, at Cana,
  you give a gentle hint:
"But even now I know that God
  will give you what you want."

Beneath that hint lies your confidence
  that Jesus loves your brother—
loves him enough to raise him up,
  if that is indeed God's will.

Thank you, Martha, for eliciting
  Jesus' striking promise:
"Those who believe in me will live,
  even though they die.
Those who believe in me will live—
  live eternally!"

O Jesus, I believe in you;
  with Martha I do believe
you are Messiah, Son of God,
  the one who gives true life.
O Jesus, I believe in you
  and in your saving word:
"I am resurrection and true life;
  whoever believes in me will live!"

Jesus Weeps for Us

Jn 11:28-37: *When she had said this, she went back and called her sister Mary, and told her privately, "The Teacher is here and is calling for you." And when she heard it, she got up quickly and went to him. Now Jesus had not yet come to the village, but was still at the place where Martha had met him. The Jews who were with her in the house, consoling her, saw Mary get up quickly and go out. They followed her because they thought that she was going to the tomb to weep there. When Mary came where Jesus was and saw him, she knelt at his feet and said to him, "Lord, if you had been here, my brother would not have died." When Jesus saw her weeping, and the Jews who came with her also weeping, he was greatly disturbed in spirit and deeply moved. He said, "Where have you laid him?" They said to him, "Lord, come and see." Jesus began to weep. So the Jews said, "See how he loved him!" But some of them said, "Could not he who opened the eyes of the blind man have kept this man from dying?"*

To contemplate:

They exclaim, "See how he loved him!"
    Your tears, O Lord, your heartfelt tears,
tell them so much more than myriad words
    about your love for him.

Your tears accompany Mary's tears
    in heartfelt sympathy—
tears of love beyond all words,
    tears of God's own Son.

O Jesus, do you suffer with us
    in your deep empathy?
O Jesus, do you weep with us
    when we cry out for your help?

In your spontaneous human emotion
    you reveal your Father-God:
our God of deep abiding love,
    who grieves with his grieving child.

"Couldn't he who opened the blind man's eyes
    have kept this man from dying?"
Ah, yes, but if he had done this,
    would we have known his love?

Love beyond all the depths of love
    that we have ever known,
love of the very Son of God
    for all his dying sheep.
Lord, love me with this love!

Lazarus, Come Out!

Jn 11:38-44: *Then Jesus, again greatly disturbed, came to the tomb. It was a cave, and a stone was lying against it. Jesus said, "Take away the stone." Martha, the sister of the dead man, said to him, "Lord, already there is a stench because he has been dead four days." Jesus said to her, "Did I not tell you that if you believed, you would see the glory of God?" So they took away the stone. And Jesus looked upward and said, "Father, I thank you for having heard me. I knew that you always hear me, but I have said this for the sake of the crowd standing here, so that they may believe that you sent me." When he had said this, he cried with a loud voice, "Lazarus, come out!" The dead man came out, his hands and feet bound with strips of cloth, and his face wrapped in a cloth. Jesus said to them, "Unbind him, and let him go."*

To contemplate:

There stands Jesus before the tomb,
   his tunic in the breeze.
Martha and Mary watch his eyes,
   intent upon the tomb.

"Roll back the stone," he cries;
    all press forward
to see whatever will happen now,
    tense with expectancy.

He speaks a prayer to his Father-God,
    a prayer of thankfulness.
But nothing has happened to be thankful for,
    nothing has changed at all.

He stakes his claim to be God's Son
    on this one moment now.
He cries aloud, "O Lazarus—
    Lazarus, come out!"

And the dead man hears and rises up;
    somehow he totters out.
He who was dead is now alive,
    standing for all to see!

More shattering than the quake of earth,
    this moment of utter calm;
more moving than a lightning bolt,
    this living corpse so still.

O Jesus, Lord of resurrection
    raise us face to face with you!

Jesus Must Die for the People

Jn 11:45-54: *Many of the Jews therefore, who had come with Mary and had seen what Jesus did, believed in him. But some of them went to the Pharisees and told them what he had done. So the chief priests and the Pharisees called a meeting of the council, and said, "What are we to do? This man is performing many signs. If we let him go on like this, everyone will believe in him, and the Romans will come and destroy both our holy place and our nation." But one of them, Caiaphas, who was high priest that year, said to them, "You know nothing at all! You do not understand that it is better for you to have one man die for the people than to have the whole nation destroyed." He did not say this on his own, but being high priest that year he prophesied that Jesus was about to die for the nation, and not for the nation only, but to gather into one the dispersed children of God. So from that day on they planned to put him to death.*

Jesus therefore no longer walked about openly among the Jews, but went from there to a town called Ephraim in the region near the wilderness; and he remained there with the disciples.

To contemplate:

Because he speaks as the high priest,
   Caiaphas speaks for God—
      but he knows it not.

Through his twisted argument
   the Spirit prophesies
      Jesus will die for all.

His death may satisfy great Rome,
   delay the coming disaster—
      the fall of Jerusalem.

But John sees something deeper here:
   salvation for eternity
      for all the people of God!

Oh, irony of ironies—
   for telling the complete truth
      Jesus must die for all.

For performing his many good works
   Jesus must suffer agony
      and shameful death.

O Jesus, give us fortitude
   to follow you in good,
      no matter what the cost.

Jesus Is the Anointed—The Christ

Jn 11:55-12:8: *Now the Passover of the Jews was near, and many went up from the country to Jerusalem before the Passover to purify themselves. They were looking for Jesus and were asking one another as they stood in the temple, "What do you think? Surely he will not come to the festival, will he?" Now the chief priests and the Pharisees had given orders that anyone who knew where Jesus was should let them know, so that they might arrest him.*

Six days before the Passover Jesus came to Bethany, the home of Lazarus, whom he had raised from the dead. There they gave a dinner for him. Martha served, and Lazarus was one of those at the table with him. Mary took a pound of costly perfume made of pure nard, anointed Jesus' feet, and wiped them with her hair. The house was filled with the fragrance of the perfume. But Judas Iscariot, one of his disciples (the one who was about to betray him), said, "Why was this perfume not sold for three hundred denarii and the money given to the poor?" (He said this not because he cared about the poor, but because he was a thief; he kept the common purse and used to steal what was put into it.) Jesus said, "Leave her alone. She bought it so that she might keep it for the day of my burial. You always have the poor with you, but you do not always have me."

To contemplate:

The high priest is not the only one
    who prophesies Jesus' death
        as God's Anointed One.

Mary remembers what he did
    for her brother Lazarus—
        she thanks Jesus with perfume.

Only the best will do for him;
    rich fragrance fills the house
        with worship of the Lord.

She bought it for his burial,
    poured it out upon the feet
        that will climb to Calvary.

Judas does not comprehend,
    objects to such a waste—
        Judas is a thief.

Jesus hints that when we give
    the poor our willing service,
        we are serving him.

O Jesus, God's Anointed One,
    may I serve you in them!

Hosanna to the King of Israel!

Jn 12:9-19: *When the great crowd of the Jews learned that he was there, they came not only because of Jesus but also to see Lazarus, whom he had raised from the dead. So the chief priests planned to put Lazarus to death as well, since it was on account of him that many of the Jews were deserting and were believing in Jesus.*

The next day the great crowd that had come to the festival heard that Jesus was coming to Jerusalem. So they took branches of palm trees and went out to meet him, shouting,

"Hosanna!

Blessed is the one who comes in the name of the Lord—
*   the King of Israel!"*

Jesus found a young donkey and sat on it; as it is written:

"Do not be afraid, daughter of Zion.

Look, your king is coming, sitting on a donkey's colt!"

His disciples did not understand these things at first; but when Jesus was glorified, then they remembered that these things had been written of him and had been done to him. So the crowd that had been with him when he called Lazarus out of the tomb and raised him from the dead continued to testify. It was also because they heard that he had performed this sign that the crowd went to meet him. The Pharisees then said to one another, "You see, you can do nothing. Look, the world has gone after him!"

To contemplate:

Long, long ago,
Jacob foretold
Judah's heir would ride a donkey's colt (Gen 49:11).

The Jewish crowd
fulfills his word—
it hails the rider: "King of Israel!"

Not as proud king
but humble servant,
Jesus rides upon a donkey's colt (Zech 9:9).

The leaders' fear
has been fulfilled:
the whole world follows Jesus.

Be wary, Lazarus!
It is now fatal
to be raised from death by Jesus!

O Jesus, our king,
foretold long ago,
raise us to rich new life in you!

The Hour Has Come

Jn 12:20-26: *Now among those who went up to worship at the festival were some Greeks. They came to Philip, who was from Bethsaida in Galilee, and said to him, "Sir, we wish to see Jesus." Philip went and told Andrew; then Andrew and Philip went and told Jesus. Jesus answered them, "The hour has come for the Son of Man to be glorified. Very truly, I tell you, unless a grain of wheat falls into the earth and dies, it remains just a single grain; but if it dies, it bears much fruit. Those who love their life lose it, and those who hate their life in this world will keep it for eternal life. Whoever serves me must follow me, and where I am, there will my servant be also. Whoever serves me, the Father will honor."*

To contemplate:

Jesus sees the Gentiles' approach
  as a sign that his "hour" has come—
  the hour he's longing for.

Long, long ago, Isaiah foretold
   God's servant would be a light
   of salvation to all the nations (Is 49:6).

But how can this be a glorious hour
   when Jesus, as grain of wheat,
   must fall into earth and die?

How can this be a glorious hour
   when Jesus must lose his life,
   on a cross on Calvary hill?

"Those who love their life will lose it!"
   How can he say such a thing?
   How can he *want* such a thing?

Of us who would serve him he demands
   we follow him even to death,
   even to Calvary!

If the grain dies, it bears much fruit—
   if Jesus dies, he bears fruit;
   if we die for him, we bear fruit.

O Jesus, we embrace this mystery,
   for you have pointed the way,
   the way to your salvation.

O Jesus, help us die with you!

I Will Draw All People to Myself

Jn 12:27-36: *"Now my soul is troubled. And what should I say— 'Father, save me from this hour'? No, it is for this reason that I have come to this hour. Father, glorify your name." Then a voice came from heaven, "I have glorified it, and I will glorify it again." The crowd standing there heard it and said that it was thunder. Others said, "An angel has spoken to him." Jesus answered, "This voice has come for your sake, not for mine. Now is the judgment of this world; now the ruler of this world will be driven out. And I, when I am lifted up from the earth, will draw all people to myself." He said this to indicate the kind of death he was to die. The crowd answered him, "We have heard from the law that the Messiah remains forever. How can you say that the Son of Man must be lifted up? Who is this Son of Man?" Jesus said to them, "The light is with you for a little longer. Walk while you have the light, so that the darkness may not overtake you. If you walk in the darkness, you do not know where you are going. While you have the light, believe in the light, so that you may become children of light."*

To contemplate:

O Jesus, troubled in soul,
I am often troubled, too.
Yet you would not pray,
"Father, save me from this hour!"

Do you now speak again
about the hour of your coming death?
You were born to die,
and in your death God is glorified?

O Jesus, can we believe
your Father glories in your death?
Can death accomplish anything?
Can death drive evil from the earth?
Can death draw us all to you?

And such a violent death—
lifted upon the Calvary cross!
Yet history bears you out:
your death still draws the crowd to you.

As death looms near to me,
and older year piles up on year,
I dread the menacing void
that death enfolds—its emptiness.

O Jesus, rouse my faith in you,
my faith that you have transformed death
as entry into glory!

They Did Not Believe in Him

Jn 12:36-43: *After Jesus had said this, he departed and hid from them. Although he had performed so many signs in their presence, they did not believe in him. This was to fulfill the word spoken by the prophet Isaiah:*

"Lord, who has believed our message,

and to whom has the arm of the Lord been revealed?"

And so they could not believe, because Isaiah also said,

"He has blinded their eyes and hardened their heart,

so that they might not look with their eyes,

and understand with their heart and turn—

and I would heal them."

Isaiah said this because he saw his glory and spoke about him. Nevertheless many, even of the authorities, believed in him. But because of the Pharisees they did not confess it, for fear that they would be put out of the synagogue; for they loved human glory more than the glory that comes from God.

To contemplate:

"He has blinded their eyes and hardened their heart!"
　　O John, can you quote Isaiah's word (Is 6:10)
　　　　after Jesus said:
"God so loved the world he sent his only Son"?
(Jn 3:16).

Isaiah was so astonished by his people's unbelief,
　　he could think only of God's power
　　　　as explanation—
so incomprehensible did he find it.

And John, impressed with the power of Jesus' signs,
　　can find no better solution now
　　　　to their unbelief
in Jesus' claim of oneness with his Father.

O yes, says John, there were a few who knew
　　Jesus must have come from above,
　　　　sent by his Father;
but they were afraid to profess their faith.

And is not the story much the same today—
　　do we not fear the belittling shrug
　　　　of many people,
if we openly proclaim our faith in Jesus?

O Jesus, don't let us value human glory
　　more than the glory of our God!

I Speak As the Father Has Told Me

Jn 12:44-50: *Then Jesus cried aloud: "Whoever believes in me believes not in me but in him who sent me. And whoever sees me sees him who sent me. I have come as light into the world, so that everyone who believes in me should not remain in the darkness. I do not judge anyone who hears my words and does not keep them, for I came not to judge the world, but to save the world. The one who rejects me and does not receive my word has a judge; on the last day the word that I have spoken will serve as judge, for I have not spoken on my own, but the Father who sent me has himself given me a commandment about what to say and what to speak. And I know that his commandment is eternal life. What I speak, therefore, I speak just as the Father has told me."*

To contemplate:

O Jesus, I do believe in you
    and in your word of truth;
I do believe you are the Word
    our heavenly Father sent.

I believe that in embracing you,
   I also embrace the Father;
opening my eyes to you as light,
   I see the Father's light!

I believe you did not come to judge,
   but to save us from the night;
open my mind to your infinite truth;
   open my heart to your grace.

"I do not judge the one who hears
   but does not keep my word."
Then, Lord, neither must I judge
   those who ignore your word.

The Father's command is eternal life;
   his command through you, my Lord,
will bring us from this land of grief
   to eternal joy with him!

O Jesus, the God that you reveal
   is the God of eternal love;
he loved us into temporal life,
   then sent his Word to us—

to assure us he will love us on,
   into eternal life!

The
Book of Glory

Jesus Loved His Own to the End

Jn 13:1-2: *Now before the festival of the Passover, Jesus knew that his hour had come to depart from this world and go to the Father. Having loved his own who were in the world, he loved them to the end. The devil had already put it into the heart of Judas son of Simon Iscariot to betray him.*

To contemplate:

At last your hour, Lord, your hour has come.

It is the hour you've been waiting for—
the hour of truth when all the world will know
you came from God and unto God return.

You came to bring the love of your Father-God
to all the men and women he gave to you.

You loved us more than shepherd loves his sheep,
more than Martha and Mary loved their Lazarus.

You loved their brother back again to life,
loved Martha as she served the festive meal,
loved Mary as she wiped your feet with her hair.

You loved Peter and John, Andrew and Thomas—
all the twelve, including even Judas;
you loved them to the end, the end of life.

And there you sit with them for your last meal,
and look around the table to see their eyes,
fixed on yours a last time before your death.

Only the eyes of Judas evade your gaze,
eyes possessed by greed for shining gold,
eyes about to be possessed by Satan.

O Jesus, sitting there with heart of love
and eyes brimming with your love for all—
Jesus, were you looking down the years
to see my face and look into my eyes?

O Jesus, did you see Judas-eyes in me,
or did you see my eyes reflecting love—
the love that led you straight to Calvary?

He Washed Their Feet

Jn 13:2-11: *And during supper Jesus, knowing that the Father had given all things into his hands, and that he had come from God and was going to God, got up from the table, took off his outer robe, and tied a towel around himself. Then he poured water into a basin and began to wash the disciples' feet and to wipe them with the towel that was tied around him. He came to Simon Peter, who said to him, "Lord, are you going to wash my feet?" Jesus answered, "You do not know now what I am doing, but later you will understand." Peter said to him, "You will never wash my feet." Jesus answered, "Unless I wash you, you have no share with me." Simon Peter said to him, "Lord, not my feet only but also my hands and my head!" Jesus said to him, "One who has bathed does not need to wash, except for the feet, but is entirely clean. And you are clean, though not all of you." For he knew who was to betray him; for this reason he said, "Not all of you are clean."*

To contemplate:

As the man who had come to them from God
   and was going back to him,
The Lord Jesus washed his disciples' feet
   and wiped them with his towel.

As the man who had come to him from God
   and was going back to him,
The Lord Jesus offered to wash Peter's feet;
   but Peter resisted him.

Yet when Jesus told him he needed it,
   Peter wanted a thorough cleansing;
whole-hearted Peter was always there,
   as the head of Jesus' band.

But water could not wash Judas clean,
   wash away betrayal—
not even Jesus' purging act
   could change Judas' will to sin.

Jesus, living water of God's grace,
   penetrate my heart.
Not only my feet, my outer self—
   wash my whole soul clean!

By Peter's side and not by Judas'
   I take my place for you.
Jesus, living water of God's grace,
   wash all my sins away!

Wash One Another's Feet

Jn 13:12-20: After he had washed their feet, had put on his robe, and had returned to the table, he said to them, "Do you know what I have done to you? You call me Teacher and Lord—and you are right, for that is what I am. So if I, your Lord and Teacher, have washed your feet, you also ought to wash one another's feet. For I have set you an example, that you also should do as I have done to you. Very truly, I tell you, servants are not greater than their master, nor are messengers greater than the one who sent them. If you know these things, you are blessed if you do them. I am not speaking of all of you; I know whom I have chosen. But it is to fulfill the scripture, 'The one who ate my bread has lifted his heel against me.' I tell you this now, before it occurs, so that when it does occur, you may believe that I am he. Very truly, I tell you, whoever receives one whom I send receives me; and whoever receives me receives him who sent me."

To contemplate:

"For I have set you an example;
   do as I have done."
Lord, through your body you touch our souls;
   through our bodies may we touch "souls."

You stoop to wash our lowly feet,
   with meekness touch our hearts.
Lord, teach us the way of humility
   to touch our neighbors' hearts!

Be our teacher, Jesus, Lord,
   teach us to follow you;
teach us the way to happiness,
   in serving others too.

Jesus, you washed Judas' feet,
   feet of treachery!
Can we, too, wash the feet of those
   who'd lift a heel against us?

Did you offer Judas your body,
   knowing he'd betray you?
Could we give our bread to those
   who'd destroy our bodies too?

O Lord, you ask too much of us;
   we cannot heroes be.
Yet, Lord, you ask much less of us
   than you yourself did give!

And It Was Night

Jn 13:21-30: *After saying this Jesus was troubled in spirit, and declared, "Very truly, I tell you, one of you will betray me." The disciples looked at one another, uncertain of whom he was speaking. One of his disciples—the one whom Jesus loved—was reclining next to him; Simon Peter therefore motioned to him to ask Jesus of whom he was speaking. So while reclining next to Jesus, he asked him, "Lord, who is it?" Jesus answered, "It is the one to whom I give this piece of bread when I have dipped it in the dish." So when he had dipped the piece of bread, he gave it to Judas son of Simon Iscariot. After he received the piece of bread, Satan entered into him. Jesus said to him, "Do quickly what you are going to do." Now no one at the table knew why he said this to him. Some thought that, because Judas had the common purse, Jesus was telling him, "Buy what we need for the festival"; or, that he should give something to the poor. So, after receiving the piece of bread, he immediately went out. And it was night.*

To contemplate:

Ah, Jesus, you had reason to be troubled—
  one of yours was ready to betray you!

Yet one there was, one you deeply loved,
  one reclining very close to you,
a confidant of your leader, Simon Peter,
  who'd take bold steps to thwart such treachery.

But it is you, dear Lord, who thwart release
  from the grip of Judas' grave disloyalty;
you clearly signal Judas as betrayer,
  yet cover up his leaving with excuse.

You offer him a piece of your own bread;
  he takes it with intent to now betray—
Satan enters into his heart and soul,
  and uses him as his own instrument.

Confused, the eleven take not a single step
  to stop Judas from his evil work;
He leaves with pretense to do some good,
  but with a heart set on betrayal.

Ah, Lord, why did you cover up his sin?
  Why prevent Peter and his faithful crew
from taking action to prevent the evil
  that lurked in Judas' heart?
Dear Lord, help me side with loving John,
  stay by you as the faithful one you love!

By Your Love They Will Know You

Jn 13:31-38: *When he had gone out, Jesus said, "Now the Son of Man has been glorified, and God has been glorified in him. If God has been glorified in him, God will also glorify him in himself and will glorify him at once. Little children, I am with you only a little longer. You will look for me; and as I said to the Jews so now I say to you, 'Where I am going, you cannot come.' I give you a new commandment, that you love one another. Just as I have loved you, you also should love one another. By this everyone will know that you are my disciples, if you have love for one another."*

Simon Peter said to him, "Lord, where are you going?" Jesus answered, "Where I am going, you cannot follow me now; but you will follow afterward." Peter said to him, "Lord, why can I not follow you now? I will lay down my life for you." Jesus answered, "Will you lay down your life for me? Very truly, I tell you, before the cock crows, you will have denied me three times."

To contemplate:

O Son of Man, how glorified?
    What kind of glory, death?
How can your Father-God take joy
    in the death of his own Son?

What kind of God glories in death—
    the death of his only Son?
What kind of barbaric deity
    do you present to us?

Yet now that Judas has gone his way
    into an evil night,
now you sit there joyfully,
    with those for whom you'll die.

You tell them of undying love:
    your love for them, theirs for you—
love that will be a vivid sign
    that they belong to you.

Peter declares he loves till death;
    you disillusion him.
Though he'll deny you three times,
    you'll go to your death for him.

O Jesus, you are no savage chief;
    your Father, no savage God!
You are our truly selfless Lord;
    Your Father, magnanimous God!

I Am the Way, and
the Truth, and the Life

Jn 14:1-7: *"Do not let your hearts be troubled. Believe in God, believe also in me. In my Father's house there are many dwelling places. If it were not so, would I have told you that I go to prepare a place for you? And if I go and prepare a place for you, I will come again and will take you to myself, so that where I am, there you may be also. And you know the way to the place where I am going."* Thomas said to him, *"Lord, we do not know where you are going. How can we know the way?"* Jesus said to him, *"I am the way, and the truth, and the life. No one comes to the Father except through me. If you know me, you will know my Father also. From now on you do know him and have seen him."*

To contemplate:

"Do not let your hearts be troubled."
   Lord, how can we not be troubled,
when you keep speaking of leaving us,
   of leaving us in death?

"Believe in God; believe in me."
  Lord, we want to believe in you,
but we do not know the way you go,
  nor the place of which you speak.

"I will prepare a place for you,
  a place in my Father's house."
If we do not know your Father's house,
  how can we know the way?

"I am the *way*, the truth, the life."
  O Lord, the way you go
is a dangerous way, the way to death!
  We're afraid to go that way.

"I am the way, the *truth*, the life."
  O Lord, the truth you tell
is a dangerous truth of life and death.
  We're afraid to hold your truth.

"I am the way, the truth, the *life!*"
  O Lord, the life you lead
is a dangerous life that leads to death.
  How can we live in death?

"Believe in God; believe in me."
  Lord, I do believe in you—
  blindly believe in you!

Whoever Has Seen Me
Has Seen My Father

Jn 14:8-14: *Philip said to him, "Lord, show us the Father, and we will be satisfied." Jesus said to him, "Have I been with you all this time, Philip, and you still do not know me? Whoever has seen me has seen the Father. How can you say, 'Show us the Father'? Do you not believe that I am in the Father and the Father is in me? The words that I say to you I do not speak on my own; but the Father who dwells in me does his works. Believe me that I am in the Father and the Father is in me; but if you do not, then believe me because of the works themselves. Very truly, I tell you, the one who believes in me will also do the works that I do and, in fact, will do greater works than these, because I am going to the Father. I will do whatever you ask in my name, so that the Father may be glorified in the Son. If in my name you ask me for anything, I will do it."*

To contemplate:

Philip, thanks for your pointed question.
  It is our question, too.
Lord, your answer is pure mystery:
  "Whoever sees me, sees the Father, too."

Are you then your own Father, Lord?
  How can you and he be one?
If you are in your Father-God,
  how can he be in you?

"My words are the Father's words in me;
  I live in him and he in me."
Lord, you tease us with mystery—
  how can your words be his?

"Believe me because of my works,
  and you will do greater works."
Lord, your works are prodigious feats—
  even raising Lazarus!

"I'll do whatever you ask of me,
  and thus glorify my Father."
Lord, will you really do so much,
  answer all our prayers?

"If in my name you ask of me,
  I will do it just for you."
Lord, I ask in your name "Jesus"
  a faith wholly in you,
the belief you are my way and truth—
  even my very life!

The Father Will Give You Another Advocate

Jn 14:15-24: *"If you love me, you will keep my commandments. And I will ask the Father, and he will give you another Advocate, to be with you forever. This is the Spirit of truth, whom the world cannot receive, because it neither sees him nor knows him. You know him, because he abides with you, and he will be in you.*

"I will not leave you orphaned; I am coming to you. In a little while the world will no longer see me, but you will see me; because I live, you also will live. On that day you will know that I am in my Father, and you in me, and I in you. They who have my commandments and keep them are those who love me; and those who love me will be loved by my Father, and I will love them and reveal myself to them." Judas (not Iscariot) said to him, *"Lord, how is it that you will reveal yourself to us, and not to the world?"* Jesus answered him, *"Those who love me will keep my word, and my Father will love them, and we will come to them and make our home with them. Whoever does not love me does not keep my words; and the word that you hear is not mine, but is from the Father who sent me."*

To contemplate:

"If you love me you will wholly keep my word—
my new commandment of love for one another."

Lord, we love you, yet we fail to keep your word.

"I will ask the Father to send you the Holy Spirit,
the Spirit of truth to be your Advocate,
to abide with you and live the truth in you."

O Jesus, are you leaving us alone?
How can we live without you, true to you?
How can this Spirit substitute for you?

"I will return to you and fully live in you;
as I live in the Father, I will live in you,
and you will live in me with my Holy Spirit."

How can you live in us, yet not in the world?

"The world rejects my word; but if you keep it,
the Father and I and the Holy Spirit will come
and make our home within your loving heart."

O Jesus, how can I fail to keep your word
when you promise such a wonderful reward?
O Father, come with Jesus into my heart!
O Holy Spirit, come, too, with your grace!
O Triune God, dwell in love with me!

I Give You My Peace

Jn 14:25-31: *"I have said these things to you while I am still with you. But the Advocate, the Holy Spirit, whom the Father will send in my name, will teach you everything, and remind you of all that I have said to you. Peace I leave with you; my peace I give to you. I do not give to you as the world gives. Do not let your hearts be troubled, and do not let them be afraid. You heard me say to you, 'I am going away, and I am coming to you.' If you loved me, you would rejoice that I am going to the Father, because the Father is greater than I. And now I have told you this before it occurs, so that when it does occur, you may believe. I will no longer talk much with you, for the ruler of this world is coming. He has no power over me; but I do as the Father has commanded me, so that the world may know that I love the Father. Rise, let us be on our way."*

To contemplate:

O Lord, we fail to keep your word;
   we are weak and we forget.

"You cannot keep my word, you say?
   My Father will send to you
the Holy Spirit to teach you how
   to do all that I've said.

"So abide in peace, the peace I give,
   the peace of the Holy Spirit—
not the false peace of this poor world,
   not the peace that rests in things.

"I am going to my Father's side,
   but I'll return to you;
so rejoice for me in my Father's house,
   and do not be afraid."

O Jesus, does your leaving us
   mean you're going to your death?

"Yes, I tell you before I go,
   that you may believe in me.
Satan, prince of this world comes,
   but only with seeming power—
I submit to death to prove my love
   for my most loving Father!"

O Jesus, with what mysterious peace
   you rise to meet your death!

Abide in Me As I Abide in You

Jn 15:1-11: *"I am the true vine, and my Father is the vinegrower. He removes every branch in me that bears no fruit. Every branch that bears fruit he prunes to make it bear more fruit. You have already been cleansed by the word that I have spoken to you. Abide in me as I abide in you. Just as the branch cannot bear fruit by itself unless it abides in the vine, neither can you unless you abide in me. I am the vine, you are the branches. Those who abide in me and I in them bear much fruit, because apart from me you can do nothing. Whoever does not abide in me is thrown away like a branch and withers; such branches are gathered, thrown into the fire, and burned. If you abide in me, and my words abide in you, ask for whatever you wish, and it will be done for you. My Father is glorified by this, that you bear much fruit and become my disciples. As the Father has loved me, so I have loved you; abide in my love. If you keep my commandments, you will abide in my love, just as I have kept my Father's commandments and abide in his love. I have said these things to you so that my joy may be in you, and that your joy may be complete."*

To contemplate:

"I am the vine, and you are the branches;
   my Father is the vinegrower.
He breaks off every branch that's dead
   and trims the ones that live."

O Jesus, how can we truly live—
   how escape dark death?

"Abide in me as I abide in you—
   then you will truly live;
my life will flow within your life,
   produce abundant fruit."

Lord, how do we abide in you?
   How do we bear fruit?

"You abide in me if you keep my word;
   thus you please my Father.
Ask him, then, whatever you need;
   he will give it to you.

"As my Father loves me, so I love you;
   live in love with me.
Keep my word as I keep his word,
   and you will live in me."

O Jesus, what joy to live in love—
   what joy to live in you!

I Command You
to Love One Another

Jn 15:9-17: *"As the Father has loved me, so I have loved you; abide in my love....*

"This is my commandment, that you love one another as I have loved you. No one has greater love than this, to lay down one's life for one's friends. You are my friends if you do what I command you. I do not call you servants any longer, because the servant does not know what the master is doing; but I have called you friends, because I have made known to you everything that I have heard from my Father. You did not choose me but I chose you. And I appointed you to go and bear fruit, fruit that will last, so that the Father will give you whatever you ask him in my name. I am giving you these commands so that you may love one another."

To contemplate:

"As the Father loves me, so I have loved you.
　　And this is what I command:
Love one another as I have loved you—
　　I have loved you unto death!"

O Jesus, no one has loved as you!
  And you command such love of us—
to love one another as your Father loves you,
  his one and only Son?

"Because you're my friends, not just my servants,
  I have confided in you.
You've not chosen me, I have chosen you
  to bear everlasting fruit."

O Jesus, you have made me your friend—
  how grateful I truly am!
You have chosen me to be your own friend.
  What fruit am I to bear?

"Fruit that will last for eternity,
  the fruit of love divine—
the creative love that made the world,
  the love that made you mine.
Your Father will give you the love you need,
  if you ask it in my name!"

O Father, *my* Father, in Jesus' name
  I longingly ask of you
the love with which you fashioned me,
  the love that sent me Jesus.
O Father, give me your love for him;
  give me his love for you!

If You Are Mine,
the World Will Hate You

Jn 15:18-25: *"If the world hates you, be aware that it hated me before it hated you. If you belonged to the world, the world would love you as its own. Because you do not belong to the world, but I have chosen you out of the world—therefore the world hates you. Remember the word that I said to you, 'Servants are not greater than their master.' If they persecuted me, they will persecute you; if they kept my word, they will keep yours also. But they will do all these things to you on account of my name, because they do not know him who sent me. If I had not come and spoken to them, they would not have sin; but now they have no excuse for their sin. Whoever hates me hates my Father also. If I had not done among them the works that no one else did, they would not have sin. But now they have seen and hated both me and my Father. It was to fulfill the word that is written in their law, 'They hated me without a cause.'"*

To contemplate:

Often now, it seems, my Lord,
   that I am out of step
with the way the world would have me think,
   and how it would have me act.

I turn to you to guide me true,
   through your Holy Spirit;
and I recall these words of yours:
   "The world will hate you, too."

O Lord, I know that if I'm yours,
   the world will not love me.
No, I must give up my timid hope
   of acceptance by the world.

"They hated me without a cause,
   and so will they hate you."

Lord, how can I bear the cross's weight—
   how can I bear *your cross?*

There is so much hate in this, our world,
   so much depressing hate.
I would escape it if I could,
   and still be true to you.

But you will never change your way—
   not for all the world!

And I will never forsake you, Lord—
   not for all the world!

I Will Send You the Spirit
of Truth from the Father

Jn 15:26-16:4: *"When the Advocate comes, whom I will send to you from the Father, the Spirit of truth who comes from the Father, he will testify on my behalf. You also are to testify because you have been with me from the beginning.*

"I have said these things to you to keep you from stumbling. They will put you out of the synagogues. Indeed, an hour is coming when those who kill you will think that by doing so they are offering worship to God. And they will do this because they have not known the Father or me. But I have said these things to you so that when their hour comes you may remember that I told you about them."

To contemplate:

"I will not leave you alone
　　to face the world.
I'll send you an Advocate
　　from my Father.

"This Spirit of truth will testify
   that I am the truth itself.
The Spirit will fill you with my truth
   to help you face the world."

O Lord, I want to tell the world
   the whole truth about you.
But I am a weak and stumbling fool,
   I quake before the cross.

O Father, send me your Spirit true,
   to brace me against the world;
send me Jesus' Holy Spirit
   to help me tell the truth.

O Holy Spirit of Jesus Christ,
   fill my mind with his holy truth,
fill my heart with his holy love—
   remake me in his image.

O Father, Son, and Holy Spirit,
   in your name I must stand.
In your name I will face the world
   and strive to tell the truth.

In your name I will testify
   to him who *is the truth!*

The Spirit Will Guide
You into All Truth

Jn 16:4-15: *"I did not say these things to you from the beginning, because I was with you. But now I am going to him who sent me; yet none of you asks me, 'Where are you going?' But because I have said these things to you, sorrow has filled your hearts. Nevertheless I tell you the truth: it is to your advantage that I go away, for if I do not go away, the Advocate will not come to you; but if I go, I will send him to you. And when he comes, he will prove the world wrong about sin and righteousness and judgment: about sin, because they do not believe in me; about righteousness, because I am going to the Father and you will see me no longer; about judgment, because the ruler of this world has been condemned.*

"I still have many things to say to you, but you cannot bear them now. When the Spirit of truth comes, he will guide you into all the truth; for he will not speak on his own, but will speak whatever he hears, and he will declare to you the things that are to come. He will glorify me, because he will take what is mine and declare it to you. All that the Father has is mine. For this reason I said that he will take what is mine and declare it to you."

To contemplate:

The world committed consummate sin
    by judging its Creator-Lord,
condemning him for his righteousness,
    and putting him to death!

Is our world really any better now—
    our world that sees no sin,
calls evil good and good a bore,
    and judges by facade?

Our world believes not in the truth,
    ignores him who is the truth;
Our world loves not the Holy Spirit,
    scoffs at his inward way.

Yet we believe you sent him, Lord,
    sent him from the Father
to lead us to the truth we need
    to find our way to you.

O Spirit of Jesus, Spirit true,
    guide us through this world,
loving all its inhabitants,
    avoiding its evil traps.
O Spirit true to our Lord the truth,
    guide us home to him—
home to the Father's house with you,
    to share everlasting bliss!

Ask in My Name

Jn 16:16-24: *"A little while, and you will no longer see me, and again a little while, and you will see me."* Then some of his disciples said to one another, *"What does he mean by saying to us, 'A little while, and you will no longer see me, and again a little while, and you will see me'; and 'Because I am going to the Father'?"* They said, *"What does he mean by this 'a little while'? We do not know what he is talking about."* Jesus knew that they wanted to ask him, so he said to them, *"Are you discussing among yourselves what I meant when I said, 'A little while, and you will no longer see me, and again a little while, and you will see me'? Very truly, I tell you, you will weep and mourn, but the world will rejoice; you will have pain, but your pain will turn into joy. When a woman is in labor, she has pain, because her hour has come. But when her child is born, she no longer remembers the anguish because of the joy of having brought a human being into the world. So you have pain now; but I will see you again, and your hearts will rejoice, and no one will take your joy from you. On that day you will ask nothing of me. Very truly, I tell you, if you ask anything of the Father in my name, he will give it to you. Until now you have not asked for anything in*

my name. Ask and you will receive, so that your joy may be complete."

To contemplate:

A little while, a little while we wait,
 and then he'll come for us!

Like the woman who waits for her new child,
 we wait in longing hope.

We've lived long enough to know joy comes
 only after sorrow and pain.

For pain is the grindstone that sharpens joy
 by contrasting preparation.

When he comes again, there's nothing we'll need!
 Till then, our need must grow.

Father, Jesus said you'll give us
 whatever we ask in his name.

And so I presume to ask one thing:
 the grace to follow him.

One grace more, my loving Father:
 your Spirit to guide my way!

I Have Conquered the World

Jn 16:25-33: *"I have said these things to you in figures of speech. The hour is coming when I will no longer speak to you in figures, but will tell you plainly of the Father. On that day you will ask in my name. I do not say to you that I will ask the Father on your behalf; for the Father himself loves you, because you have loved me and have believed that I came from God. I came from the Father and have come into the world; again, I am leaving the world and am going to the Father."*

His disciples said, "Yes, now you are speaking plainly, not in any figure of speech! Now we know that you know all things, and do not need to have anyone question you; by this we believe that you came from God." Jesus answered them, "Do you now believe? The hour is coming, indeed it has come, when you will be scattered, each one to his home, and you will leave me alone. Yet I am not alone because the Father is with me. I have said this to you, so that in me you may have peace. In the world you face persecution. But take courage; I have conquered the world!"

To contemplate:

"The Father himself loves you,
because you have loved me
and have believed in me."

Yes, Jesus, we have loved you
and have believed in you—
you are our truth and our life!

O Father, Jesus reveals
a deep, eternal mystery:
your love for us your children.

And that even deeper mystery:
his return to life with you,
return to eternal life.

As disciples we believe;
yet he warns us not to trust
in our own, so fragile faith.

Even should we abandon him
you, Father, will forgive us
and dwell in us in peace.

O Jesus, you conquered the world—
for us you conquered Satan,
and opened heaven's joy!

Father, the Hour Has Come

Jn 17:1-10: *After Jesus had spoken these words, he looked up to heaven and said, "Father, the hour has come; glorify your Son so that the Son may glorify you, since you have given him authority over all people, to give eternal life to all whom you have given him. And this is eternal life, that they may know you, the only true God, and Jesus Christ whom you have sent. I glorified you on earth by finishing the work that you gave me to do. So now, Father, glorify me in your own presence with the glory that I had in your presence before the world existed.*

"I have made your name known to those whom you gave me from the world. They were yours, and you gave them to me, and they have kept your word. Now they know that everything you have given me is from you; for the words that you gave to me I have given to them, and they have received them and know in truth that I came from you; and they have believed that you sent me. I am asking on their behalf; I am not asking on behalf of the world, but on behalf of those whom you gave me, because they are yours. All mine are yours, and yours are mine; and I have been glorified in them."

To contemplate:

O Jesus, thank you for these words,
    intimate words to your Father—
words that reveal you as his Word
    and him as our ultimate source.

Thank you for words of eternal life,
    the life we hope to share
with you in glory everlasting,
    in presence of our Father.

You reveal that we belong to God,
    you reveal him as our Father—
a Father who gave us all to you,
    that we may keep your word.

O Father, thank you for sending him
    who speaks such words to you—
your own dear Son to speak of you,
    and be your Word to us.

Thank you for sending your only Son
    to give his life for us;
thanks for this, his hour of glory—
    his hour of sacrifice.

Help us give ourselves wholly to him,
    that we may belong to you!

As You Have Sent Me, I Send Them

Jn 17:11-19: *"And now I am no longer in the world, but they are in the world, and I am coming to you. Holy Father, protect them in your name that you have given me, so that they may be one, as we are one. While I was with them, I protected them in your name that you have given me. I guarded them, and not one of them was lost except the one destined to be lost, so that the scripture might be fulfilled. But now I am coming to you, and I speak these things in the world so that they may have my joy made complete in themselves. I have given them your word, and the world has hated them because they do not belong to the world, just as I do not belong to the world. I am not asking you to take them out of the world, but I ask you to protect them from the evil one. They do not belong to the world, just as I do not belong to the world. Sanctify them in the truth; your word is truth. As you have sent me into the world, so I have sent them into the world. And for their sakes I sanctify myself, so that they also may be sanctified in truth."*

To contemplate:

"Father, I am now coming to you."
  O Jesus, don't leave us alone!

"Father, protect them in your name."
  O Jesus, you inspire our trust!

"That they may be one, as we are one."
  O Jesus, you stir up our love!

"While I was with them, I protected them."
  O Jesus, your word is truth!

"I guarded them, and not one was lost."
  O Jesus, what a word of peace!

"I speak these words that they may have joy."
  O Jesus, you *are* our joy!

"The world hates them, for they don't belong."
  O Jesus, we belong to you!

"Father, protect them from all evil."
  O Jesus, you pray for us!

"Sanctify them in your sacred truth."
  O Jesus, you make us holy!

"For their sakes I sanctify myself."
  O Jesus, you *are* our hope!

That You May Be One

Jn 17:20-26: *"I ask not only on behalf of these, but also on behalf of those who will believe in me through their word, that they may all be one. As you, Father, are in me and I am in you, may they also be in us, so that the world may believe that you have sent me. The glory that you have given me I have given them, so that they may be one, as we are one, I in them and you in me, that they may become completely one, so that the world may know that you have sent me and have loved them even as you have loved me. Father, I desire that those also, whom you have given me, may be with me where I am, to see my glory, which you have given me because you loved me before the foundation of the world.*

"Righteous Father, the world does not know you, but I know you; and these know that you have sent me. I made your name known to them, and I will make it known, so that the love with which you have loved me may be in them, and I in them."

To contemplate:

One—all true Christians,
   who hear your prayer,
      must be *one in you!*

Yet we are not one—
   not one in faith,
      not one in love!

Can we live in you and you in us,
   if we cannot live
      with one another?

Can we unite in your joy
   as long as we stay
      divided in heart?

Can the world ever know
   you and the Father are one,
      if we are not one?

O Jesus, pray for us now
   as you did then—
      that we may be one.

Take us into your heart,
   to be one with you
      and with our Father.

Lord, give us the love
   with which you love!

I Am He

Jn 18:1-11: *After Jesus had spoken these words, he went out with his disciples across the Kidron valley to a place where there was a garden, which he and his disciples entered. Now Judas, who betrayed him, also knew the place, because Jesus often met there with his disciples. So Judas brought a detachment of soldiers together with police from the chief priests and the Pharisees, and they came there with lanterns and torches and weapons. Then Jesus, knowing all that was to happen to him, came forward and asked them, "Whom are you looking for?" They answered, "Jesus of Nazareth." Jesus replied, "I am he." Judas, who betrayed him, was standing with them. When Jesus said to them, "I am he," they stepped back and fell to the ground. Again he asked them, "Whom are you looking for?" And they said, "Jesus of Nazareth." Jesus answered, "I told you that I am he. So if you are looking for me, let these men go." This was to fulfill the word that he had spoken, "I did not lose a single one of those whom you gave me." Then Simon Peter, who had a sword, drew it, struck the high priest's slave, and cut off his right ear. The slave's name was Malchus. Jesus said to Peter, "Put your sword back into*

its sheath. Am I not to drink the cup that the Father has given me?"

To contemplate:

They come with torches and weapons.
   You know the terrible things they'll do;
      yet you advance to meet them.

With only your word, you, the Word,
   flatten them in their tracks;
      for you are he—*Yahweh!*

Your "I am he" echoes God's "I Am" (Ex 3:14).
   They fall down in a faint;
      they cannot stand your truth.

In this great moment of truth
   you defend your little band,
      and the soldiers let them go.

But impetuous Peter draws his sword
   and strikes a mighty blow—
      cuts off a poor slave's ear.

Peter must learn your gentle way,
   renounce his impulsive path
      and drink the Father's cup.

O Lord, my gentle Jesus Christ,
   teach me your way of love—
      even for enemies!

Jesus Lets Them Arrest
and Bind Him

Jn 18:12-18: *So the soldiers, their officer, and the Jewish police arrested Jesus and bound him. First they took him to Annas, who was the father-in-law of Caiaphas, the high priest that year. Caiaphas was the one who had advised the Jews that it was better to have one person die for the people.*

Simon Peter and another disciple followed Jesus. Since that disciple was known to the high priest, he went with Jesus into the courtyard of the high priest, but Peter was standing outside at the gate. So the other disciple, who was known to the high priest, went out, spoke to the woman who guarded the gate, and brought Peter in. The woman said to Peter, "You are not also one of this man's disciples, are you?" He said, "I am not." Now the slaves and the police had made a charcoal fire because it was cold, and they were standing around it and warming themselves. Peter also was standing with them and warming himself.

To contemplate:

The Lord of this great universe
   they arrest and even bind,
      to be judged by puny men.

O Lord of this great universe
   we judge you again today—
      you are guilty of loving us!

They take you then to Annas,
   the father of Caiaphas,
      who has already judged you:

"Better to have one person die,"
   Caiaphas had cried:
      "Much better he, than we."

But Peter has not fled away;
   he and one other disciple
      have followed Jesus in.

The woman guarding the outer gate
   challenges poor Peter—
      and he denies his Lord.

Ah, Peter, warm yourself full well,
   for it is cold outside—
      yet colder in your heart!

Lord, how often we stand outside—
   outside your loving heart!

I Have Spoken Openly to the World

Jn 18:19-28: *Then the high priest questioned Jesus about his disciples and about his teaching. Jesus answered, "I have spoken openly to the world; I have always taught in synagogues and in the temple, where all the Jews come together. I have said nothing in secret. Why do you ask me? Ask those who heard what I said to them; they know what I said." When he had said this, one of the police standing nearby struck Jesus on the face, saying, "Is that how you answer the high priest?" Jesus answered, "If I have spoken wrongly, testify to the wrong. But if I have spoken rightly, why do you strike me?" Then Annas sent him bound to Caiaphas the high priest.*

Now Simon Peter was standing and warming himself. They asked him, "You are not also one of his disciples, are you?" He denied it and said, "I am not." One of the slaves of the high priest, a relative of the man whose ear Peter had cut off, asked, "Did I not see you in the garden with him?" Again Peter denied it, and at that moment the cock crowed.

To contemplate:

Jesus laid down an extreme demand:
  "Love each other as I love you" (15:12).
Such love could not be allowed to live—
  who knows where it might lead?

In his Sermon out upon the Mount
  Jesus had made another demand:
"If anyone strikes you upon the cheek,
  turn the other one, too" (Mt 5:39).

The guard strikes Jesus upon the cheek—
  does he turn the other, too?
No, he invites the guard to be a man
  who thinks before he acts.

"Turn the other cheek" does not mean
  to be a coward;
rather, challenge your challengers
  to recall their dignity and yours.

Jesus stands up to his accusers,
  a man who does not cringe;
Peter crumbles at a mere question—
  three times denies his Lord.

O Jesus, give me your great courage
  to face adversity;
and give me your great love of all—
  even those who'd strike me.

Jesus Before Pilate

Jn 18:28-32: *Then they took Jesus from Caiaphas to Pilate's headquarters. It was early in the morning. They themselves did not enter the headquarters, so as to avoid ritual defilement and to be able to eat the Passover. So Pilate went out to them and said, "What accusation do you bring against this man?" They answered, "If this man were not a criminal, we would not have handed him over to you." Pilate said to them, "Take him yourselves and judge him according to your law." The Jews replied, "We are not permitted to put anyone to death." (This was to fulfill what Jesus had said when he indicated the kind of death he was to die.)*

To contemplate:

Pilate may be governor,
   but still a Gentile;
to cross his threshold is a stain,
   voiding all holy acts.

John notes the irony here—
    an innocent, holy man
is handed over to death
    but they do not see the wrong.

Do I not often act the same?
    Think small things are crimes
that would utterly disqualify
    from observance of God's law?

At the same time
    do I let weighty things pass,
forgetting that at life's end
    I will be judged on love?

Do I judge others harshly,
    think they deserve the worst
for failings that in myself
    I'd hardly think of twice?

O Jesus, Lord of Gentile and Jew,
    Jesus, my own dear Lord—
save us from hypocrisy,
    save us from ourselves!

I Came into This World
to Be Its King

Jn:18:33-40: *Then Pilate entered the headquarters again, summoned Jesus, and asked him, "Are you the King of the Jews?" Jesus answered, "Do you ask this on your own, or did others tell you about me?" Pilate replied, "I am not a Jew, am I? Your own nation and the chief priests have handed you over to me. What have you done?" Jesus answered, "My kingdom is not from this world. If my kingdom were from this world, my followers would be fighting to keep me from being handed over to the Jews. But as it is, my kingdom is not from here." Pilate asked him, "So you are a king?" Jesus answered, "You say that I am a king. For this I was born, and for this I came into the world, to testify to the truth. Everyone who belongs to the truth listens to my voice." Pilate asked him, "What is truth?"*

After he had said this, he went out to the Jews again and told them, "I find no case against him. But you have a custom that I release someone for you at the Passover. Do you want me to release for you the King of the Jews?" They shouted in reply, "Not this man, but Barabbas!" Now Barabbas was a bandit.

To contemplate:

"Are you really the King of the Jews?
    Do you claim to be their king?
If you are their king, what have you done
    to arouse such mortal hate?"

"My kingdom is not within this world;
    I am the king of another world,
a world beyond the Roman rule,
    a world above this world.

"Yes, truly I am a king,
    the king of the realm of truth.
Whoever belongs to truth itself,
    belongs to me as king."

"O pitiful man, what is truth?
    Does anyone believe in truth?
We Romans have no need of truth—
    we have our mighty arms!"

O Pilate, governor of men,
    how can you be so crass?
Yet you look for an excuse to let him go,
    excuse of festive rite.

O Jesus, king of another world,
    be my king here now!

Here Is the Man!

Jn 19:1-7: Then Pilate took Jesus and had him flogged. And the soldiers wove a crown of thorns and put it on his head, and they dressed him in a purple robe. They kept coming up to him, saying, "Hail, King of the Jews!" and striking him on the face. Pilate went out again and said to them, "Look, I am bringing him out to you to let you know that I find no case against him." So Jesus came out, wearing the crown of thorns and the purple robe. Pilate said to them, "Here is the man!" When the chief priests and the police saw him, they shouted, "Crucify him! Crucify him!" Pilate said to them, "Take him yourselves and crucify him; I find no case against him." The Jews answered him, "We have a law, and according to that law he ought to die because he has claimed to be the Son of God."

To contemplate:

Because he claims to be the truth,
    Pilate tortures him—
flogs him with heavy weighted thongs
    till his blood stains the ground.

The soldiers begin their macabre play:
    they crown his head with thorns
and dress him in a purple robe
    to mock his royal claim.

He says he is the King of Jews?
    We'll give him his just due:
we'll bloody his handsome face
    and sink his crown down deep!

Pilate brings him before the crowd,
    wearing his crown of thorns.
"I bring him to you as innocent;
    you have no case at all."

How does Pilate say the words,
    "Behold, here is the man"?
Does he say them in pity for his plight,
    or in awe at his dignity?

"Crucify him! Crucify him!"
    roars the crowd.
And Pilate gives consent,
    though he finds no cause in him.

O Jesus, I look upon your face
    and cry, "What a man you are!"

Where Are You From?

Jn 19:7-12: *"He ought to die because he has claimed to be the Son of God."*

Now when Pilate heard this, he was more afraid than ever. He entered his headquarters again and asked Jesus, "Where are you from?" But Jesus gave him no answer. Pilate therefore said to him, "Do you refuse to speak to me? Do you not know that I have power to release you, and power to crucify you?" Jesus answered him, "You would have no power over me unless it had been given you from above; therefore the one who handed me over to you is guilty of a greater sin." From then on Pilate tried to release him, but the Jews cried out, "If you release this man, you are no friend of the emperor. Everyone who claims to be a king sets himself against the emperor."

To contemplate:

"Son of God!" rouses Pilate's awe
  of the man he already holds in fear:
    "Could he really be God's Son?"

"O Jesus, where are you really from?
  Are you from another world than this,
    that world of which you spoke?"

And all of us must ask this thing;
  and all of us respond
    to this most vital question of all:
      "Where are you really from?"

Jesus already has said enough;
  his silence vexes Pilate:
    "Do you know how powerful I am?"
      "Real power is with God!"

A man who answers with such words
  is a man whom Pilate fears.
    If he should really be a king,
      who has the greater power?

Jesus, I believe you are my king;
  greater than Caesar, you!
    Jesus, I believe you are from God—
      the only Son of God!

Crucify Him!

Jn 19:12-16: *"Everyone who claims to be a king sets himself against the emperor."*

When Pilate heard these words, he brought Jesus outside and sat on the judge's bench at a place called The Stone Pavement, or in Hebrew Gabbatha. Now it was the day of Preparation for the Passover; and it was about noon. He said to the Jews, "Here is your King!" They cried out, "Away with him! Away with him! Crucify him!" Pilate asked them, "Shall I crucify your king?" The chief priests answered, "We have no king but the emperor." Then he handed him over to them to be crucified.

To contemplate:

Poor pretentious Pilate,
   sitting on judgment seat,
   giving out stern decrees,
pronounces solemn word.

"Here is your king!" says he.
　They answer with mockery:
　"No king of ours is he,
deserving of violent death!"

Poor pretentious Pilate
　knows only taunt for taunt,
　cries from his judgment seat,
"Shall I crucify *your king?*"

Though he tries to play the part
　of his most high estate,
　they know they've got him now:
"Caesar's our only king!"

Poor pretentious Pilate
　knows they lie to him.
　But how can he now escape
inevitable defeat?

He hands over the noblest man
　that he has ever seen—
gives him to the crowd he scorns,
　to do with as they wish.

O Jesus Christ, my noble Lord,
　they treat you as a pawn
in their contemptible tug-of-war.
　I adore you as my king!

They Crucified Him

Jn 19:16-25: *So they took Jesus; and carrying the cross by himself, he went out to what is called The Place of the Skull, which in Hebrew is called Golgotha. There they crucified him, and with him two others, one on either side, with Jesus between them. Pilate also had an inscription written and put on the cross. It read, "Jesus of Nazareth, the King of the Jews." Many of the Jews read this inscription, because the place where Jesus was crucified was near the city; and it was written in Hebrew, in Latin, and in Greek. Then the chief priests of the Jews said to Pilate, "Do not write, 'The King of the Jews,' but, 'This man said, I am King of the Jews.'" Pilate answered, "What I have written I have written." When the soldiers had crucified Jesus, they took his clothes and divided them into four parts, one for each soldier. They also took his tunic; now the tunic was seamless, woven in one piece from the top. So they said to one another, "Let us not tear it, but cast lots for it to see who will get it." This was to fulfill what the scripture says,*

> *"They divided my clothes among themselves,*
>   *and for my clothing they cast lots."*

And that is what the soldiers did.

To contemplate:

John's Jesus carries his cross
    to the cruel Place of the Skull—
a kingly figure to the end,
    as Pilate's inscription reads.

In sacred and in secular tongues
    he is the King of the Jews—
in fact, the king of all our race,
    even as Pilate guessed.

As the psalmist said in ancient days,
    "They divided all my clothes,
and for my vesture they cast lots" (Ps 22:18).
    They play their game with him!

And there he hangs upon his cross
    between good earth and sky—
hangs for all the world to see,
    glance up, and pass him by.

His blood drips slowly to the ground,
    his head bows ever down;
yet the world he dies for, goes right on,
    as though nothing has transpired!

O Jesus, suffering there for me,
    I stop, to gaze at you.

Here Is Your Mother

Jn 19:25-27: *Meanwhile, standing near the cross of Jesus were his mother, and his mother's sister, Mary the wife of Clopas, and Mary Magdalene. When Jesus saw his mother and the disciple whom he loved standing beside her, he said to his mother, "Woman, here is your son." Then he said to the disciple, "Here is your mother." And from that hour the disciple took her into his own home.*

To contemplate:

As he sinks downward toward his death
   to give his life for us,
he has one last and lasting gift
   besides himself—his mother!

"Woman, here is your beloved son,"
   he says to his mother—
and he points to his beloved John
   in the place of all of us.

"Woman," the title he gave to her
    when he made the Cana wine (Jn 2:4)—
"Woman," the title that John will use
    to relate her to the Church:
the cosmic "Woman clothed with the sun,
    with the moon under her feet" (Rev 12:1).

And to John and you and me he says,
    "Here is your mother."
O Jesus, no treasure is so rich
    as this gift you give to us.

The gift of your own mother,
    who heard the angel's voice
and answered with her heart of love,
    "God's will be done in me" (Lk 1:38).

Like the disciple Jesus loved,
    I would take her to my home;
O Mary, come and live with me,
    and be my mother too.

O Jesus, I cannot comprehend
    such a marvelous gift—
the mother who bore you
    you give us as our own!

He Gave Up His Spirit

Jn 19:28-30: *After this, when Jesus knew that all was now finished, he said (in order to fulfill the scripture), "I am thirsty." A jar full of sour wine was standing there. So they put a sponge full of the wine on a branch of hyssop and held it to his mouth. When Jesus had received the wine, he said, "It is finished." Then he bowed his head and gave up his spirit.*

To contemplate:

He is dying, yet he must fulfill
   the psalmist's prophecy:
"For my thirst they gave me only
   vinegar to drink" (Ps 69:21).

Obedient to the very end,
   he does his Father's will
in everything, both great and small,
   even to feeling thirst.

But the thirst he feels is an inner thirst,
    the thirst for eternal life,
the life with his Father and Holy Spirit,
    the very life of God!

The thirst he feels is an inner thirst,
    a thirst for the love of us—
the men and women to whom he gives his life,
    a share in his life with God.

Now he has finished his course on earth;
    he has done his Father's will.
Nothing more, but to give his life,
    into his Father's hands.

He gives up his body, so lean and lithe,
    gives up his head, so wise,
gives up his hands, carpenter-hands,
    gives up his servant-feet.

Jesus gives up his human spirit,
    his driving spirit of love;
into his Father's hands he returns
    all his Father gave to him.

O Jesus, you gave yourself for me—
    may I give myself to you!

Blood and Water
Flowed from His Side

Jn 19:31-37: *Since it was the day of Preparation, the Jews did not want the bodies left on the cross during the sabbath, especially because that sabbath was a day of great solemnity. So they asked Pilate to have the legs of the crucified men broken and the bodies removed. Then the soldiers came and broke the legs of the first and of the other who had been crucified with him. But when they came to Jesus and saw that he was already dead, they did not break his legs. Instead, one of the soldiers pierced his side with a spear, and at once blood and water came out. (He who saw this has testified so that you also may believe. His testimony is true, and he knows that he tells the truth.) These things occurred so that the scripture might be fulfilled, "None of his bones shall be broken." And again another passage of scripture says, "They will look on the one whom they have pierced."*

To contemplate:

O Jesus, your death prepared the way
   for your great paschal feast.
Without your death all our poor deaths
   would be meaningless.

Even the manner of your death
   fulfilled the prophecies:
as our Paschal Lamb, none of your bones
   would be broken in your death (Ex 12:46).

As our Paschal Lamb, you are the source
   of our baptismal water,
the water that flowed from your wounded side
   to refresh our thirsting souls.

As our Paschal Lamb, you are the source
   of our Eucharistic feast—
the body and blood of your sacrifice,
   our spiritual food and drink.

Now all the world can look at you,
   as Zechariah said—
"They look on the one whom they have pierced
   and mourn for an only child" (Zech 12:10).

For you are truly an only child,
   the only Son of God.

Does God, too, from his heaven above,
   mourn for his only Son?

They Placed Him in the Tomb

Jn 19:38-42: *After these things, Joseph of Arimathea, who was a disciple of Jesus, though a secret one because of his fear of the Jews, asked Pilate to let him take away the body of Jesus. Pilate gave him permission; so he came and removed his body. Nicodemus, who had at first come to Jesus by night, also came, bringing a mixture of myrrh and aloes, weighing about a hundred pounds. They took the body of Jesus and wrapped it with the spices in linen cloths, according to the burial custom of the Jews. Now there was a garden in the place where he was crucified, and in the garden there was a new tomb in which no one had ever been laid. And so, because it was the Jewish day of Preparation, and the tomb was nearby, they laid Jesus there.*

To contemplate:

O Jesus, dead upon the cross,
    dead in your mother's arms;
O Jesus, dead within the tomb,
    can you still hear my prayer?

O pioneer of the after-life,
    my precursor into death,
what is it like on the other side,
    the other side of life?

Do you know what Joseph has done for you?
    Did the myrrh and aloes help?
What do you think of your new hewn tomb
    and the garden in which it lies?

O Jesus, we know so little of death
    and what the dead perceive!
You revealed so much about our life—
    what do you tell of our death?

Our dear dead seem so far from us,
    so indifferent to our flowers
and all the attentions we pay to them—
    does our mourning help at all?

Like your disciples and holy women,
    we wonder in suspense.

Yet, with them we are confident
    that death can't end your life!

He Must Rise from the Dead

Jn 20:1-10: *Early on the first day of the week, while it was still dark, Mary Magdalene came to the tomb and saw that the stone had been removed from the tomb. So she ran and went to Simon Peter and the other disciple, the one whom Jesus loved, and said to them, "They have taken the Lord out of the tomb, and we do not know where they have laid him." Then Peter and the other disciple set out and went toward the tomb. The two were running together, but the other disciple outran Peter and reached the tomb first. He bent down to look in and saw the linen wrappings lying there, but he did not go in. Then Simon Peter came, following him, and went into the tomb. He saw the linen wrappings lying there, and the cloth that had been on Jesus' head, not lying with the linen wrappings but rolled up in a place by itself. Then the other disciple, who reached the tomb first, also went in, and he saw and believed; for as yet they did not understand the scripture, that he must rise from the dead. Then the disciples returned to their homes.*

To contemplate:

Before the stirring of the dawn
   Mary Magdalene stirs forth,
anxious to be near her Lord,
   even in his tomb.

And behold, it is no longer sealed!
   Whatever the meaning be,
Peter must be the first to know—
   Peter and John must know.

The two cannot restrain their zeal;
   they race on toward the tomb.
John, the beloved, leads the pace,
   yet courteously gives place
   of honor to Simon Peter.

But the body of Jesus is not there;
   they find only its wrappings
and the headcloth—but he is gone,
   gone they know not where.

Has someone stolen Jesus' body,
   or has he come alive?
The prophet's words were vague,
   too subtle on this point.

Yet the beloved disciple believes—
   he believes...and so do I!

"Mary!"

Jn 20:11-18: *But Mary stood weeping outside the tomb. As she wept, she bent over to look into the tomb; and she saw two angels in white, sitting where the body of Jesus had been lying, one at the head and the other at the feet. They said to her, "Woman, why are you weeping?" She said to them, "They have taken away my Lord, and I do not know where they have laid him." When she had said this, she turned around and saw Jesus standing there, but she did not know that it was Jesus. Jesus said to her, "Woman, why are you weeping? Whom are you looking for?" Supposing him to be the gardener, she said to him, "Sir, if you have carried him away, tell me where you have laid him, and I will take him away." Jesus said to her, "Mary!" She turned and said to him in Hebrew, "Rabbouni!" (which means Teacher). Jesus said to her, "Do not hold on to me, because I have not yet ascended to the Father. But go to my brothers and say to them, 'I am ascending to my Father and your Father, to my God and your God.'" Mary Magdalene went and announced to the disciples, "I have seen the Lord"; and she told them that he had said these things to her.*

To contemplate:

He died, and yet he lives!
  Jesus has passed
    the boundaries of life and death!

There he stands, a robust man,
  taken for gardener—
    no incorporeal being, he.

Though she knows him not,
  he knows her well—
    he calls her by her name.

She lays delighted hold of him,
  but he breaks free—
    earth can't hold him now.

Upward to his loving Father
  he will soon ascend,
    but first there's work to do.

He calls upon the Magdalene,
  to be the first missioner
    of good news to his apostles.

O Jesus, risen from the dead,
  send me to announce
    your good news to your people!

Peace Be with You

Jn 20:19-23: *When it was evening on that day, the first day of the week, and the doors of the house where the disciples had met were locked for fear of the Jews, Jesus came and stood among them and said, "Peace be with you." After he said this, he showed them his hands and his side. Then the disciples rejoiced when they saw the Lord. Jesus said to them again, "Peace be with you. As the Father has sent me, so I send you." When he had said this, he breathed on them and said to them, "Receive the Holy Spirit. If you forgive the sins of any, they are forgiven them; if you retain the sins of any, they are retained."*

To contemplate:

Doors of matter cannot hold him now,
	but only spiritual doors—
the doors they had closed in deep despair,
	when he hung upon the cross.

They had shut him out for fear of death
   in company with him;
and now they cringe in lonely fright,
   shutting out the world.

He comes with peace, his peace of heart,
   bearing the very wounds
that had quenched in them the hope he'd brought,
   the hope of glorious life.

The wounds by which they know him now
   were the price of the peace he brings;
and now they are the glowing gems
   of his life beyond the tomb.

He brings them peace, the peace of pardon
   for their abandoning him.
He brings them a new source of peace—
   the Holy Spirit of peace.

Not only has he forgiven them,
   he gives them his power to pardon
all who lose their peace by sin—
   pardon them in God's name.

O Jesus, bringer of holy peace,
   sender of Holy Spirit,
as the Father sent you, send us, too,
   in the Spirit's holy peace.

My Lord and My God!

Jn 20:24-31: *But Thomas (who was called the Twin), one of the twelve, was not with them when Jesus came. So the other disciples told him, "We have seen the Lord." But he said to them, "Unless I see the mark of the nails in his hands, and put my finger in the mark of the nails and my hand in his side, I will not believe."*

A week later his disciples were again in the house, and Thomas was with them. Although the doors were shut, Jesus came and stood among them and said, "Peace be with you." Then he said to Thomas, "Put your finger here and see my hands. Reach out your hand and put it in my side. Do not doubt but believe." Thomas answered him, "My Lord and my God!" Jesus said to him, "Have you believed because you have seen me? Blessed are those who have not seen and yet have come to believe."

Now Jesus did many other signs in the presence of his disciples, which are not written in this book. But these are written so that you may come to believe that Jesus is the Messiah, the Son of God, and that through believing you may have life in his name.

To contemplate:

To see your glory in the dawn
   is indeed a wondrous thing.
To see your splendor in a tree
   is a gift of tranquil joy.

But to see your glory in a wound,
   your splendor in suffering—
that is a gift beyond our ken,
   a gift of the Holy Spirit.

Thanks for your patience with doubting Thomas;
   thanks for giving him proof.
We, too, find it hard to believe in you;
   we, too, look for evidence.
Yet you bless us more deeply for simple faith,
   faith that is wholly trust;
and you give us this gift through the Holy One,
   your Holy Spirit of love.

O Jesus, to touch your wounded side,
   look into your wounded heart,
and know the depth of your suffering,
   is more than enough for us!

And do we not see your wounded heart
   in the hearts of all our race?
With Thomas we cry to your wounded heart:
   "My Lord and my wounded God!"

It Is the Lord!

Jn 21:1-8: *After these things Jesus showed himself again to the disciples by the Sea of Tiberias; and he showed himself in this way. Gathered there together were Simon Peter, Thomas called the Twin, Nathanael of Cana in Galilee, the sons of Zebedee, and two others of his disciples. Simon Peter said to them, "I am going fishing." They said to him, "We will go with you." They went out and got into the boat, but that night they caught nothing.*

Just after daybreak, Jesus stood on the beach; but the disciples did not know that it was Jesus. Jesus said to them, "Children, you have no fish, have you?" They answered him, "No." He said to them, "Cast the net to the right side of the boat, and you will find some." So they cast it, and now they were not able to haul it in because there were so many fish. That disciple whom Jesus loved said to Peter, "It is the Lord!" When Simon Peter heard that it was the Lord, he put on some clothes, for he was naked, and jumped into the sea. But the other disciples came in the boat, dragging the net full of fish, for they were not far from the land, only about a hundred yards off.

To contemplate:

All night the disciples cast their nets,
   but their work is all in vain.
Over and over they try their luck,
   but the morning finds them spent.

As "fishers of men" they will learn the same:
   no matter how hard they try,
if they cast their nets without the Lord,
   they'll cast them all in vain.

This lesson they had to learn once more,
   after years of following him:
without him they can do not a thing;
   with him, everything.

And only the disciple whom Jesus loved
   could see him on the shore;
only the disciple who loved the Lord
   could recognize his voice.

Yet impetuous Peter loves him, too,
   loves him with deep respect.
He covers himself and plunges in
   to be with him once more.

O John, give me a share in your love,
   and Peter, a share in your fire!

They Knew It Was the Lord

Jn 21:9-14: *When they had gone ashore, they saw a charcoal fire there, with fish on it, and bread. Jesus said to them, "Bring some of the fish that you have just caught." So Simon Peter went aboard and hauled the net ashore, full of large fish, a hundred fifty-three of them; and though there were so many, the net was not torn. Jesus said to them, "Come and have breakfast." Now none of the disciples dared to ask him, "Who are you?" because they knew it was the Lord. Jesus came and took the bread and gave it to them, and did the same with the fish. This was now the third time that Jesus appeared to the disciples after he was raised from the dead.*

To contemplate:

A simple lakeside scene is this—
   a picnic in the dawn,
      catered by the Lord.

He invites them to participate
   in preparing the meal;
      they have their part to play.

"Bring me some of your fish," says he;
   and Peter obeys his call,
      dragging them all ashore!

He has the fire roaring strong,
   he has fresh bread for them;
      he adds the fish they've caught.

He feeds them as he fed the crowd;
   they know him by his gifts—
      they know him by his love.

This is the third time Jesus comes
   to assure them he has risen
      and bring to them his love.

At the first he taught them to forgive,
   at the second, to believe;
      and now, to collaborate with his grace.

O Jesus, gentle Lord of love,
   come into my life, too:
      inspire me to forgive,
   to believe with all my heart,
      and be open to your grace.

Do You Love Me?

Jn 21:15-19: *When they had finished breakfast, Jesus said to Simon Peter, "Simon son of John, do you love me more than these?" He said to him, "Yes, Lord; you know that I love you." Jesus said to him, "Feed my lambs." A second time he said to him, "Simon son of John, do you love me?" He said to him, "Yes, Lord; you know that I love you." Jesus said to him, "Tend my sheep." He said to him the third time, "Simon son of John, do you love me?" Peter felt hurt because he said to him the third time, "Do you love me?" And he said to him, "Lord, you know everything; you know that I love you." Jesus said to him, "Feed my sheep. Very truly, I tell you, when you were younger, you used to fasten your own belt and to go wherever you wished. But when you grow old, you will stretch out your hands, and someone else will fasten a belt around you and take you where you do not wish to go." (He said this to indicate the kind of death by which he would glorify God.) After this he said to him, "Follow me."*

To contemplate:

Lord, when all is said and done,
  what will your question be?
You will ask, "Do you love me?"
  On the answer hinges life!

But that simple "Yes" is not enough;
  you ask again and again!
Like Peter, can we answer "Yes,
  yes, yes," again and again?

Does our whole eternity
  depend upon our love?
Does intelligence count for naught?
  And what of power of will?

We have mind and heart and will.
  Yet most depends on heart.
Mind must illuminate the heart
  and will, carry out its goal.

Yet Peter will lose his will at last,
  his freedom to come and go.
Others will lead him to his death,
  even as they did you.

O Peter, pray that we may do
  even as you have done;
that we may follow Jesus, Lord,
  follow him to the end!

Follow Me

Jn 21:20-25: *Peter turned and saw the disciple whom Jesus loved following them; he was the one who had reclined next to Jesus at the supper and had said, "Lord, who is it that is going to betray you?" When Peter saw him, he said to Jesus, "Lord, what about him?" Jesus said to him, "If it is my will that he remain until I come, what is that to you? Follow me!" So the rumor spread in the community that this disciple would not die. Yet Jesus did not say to him that he would not die, but, "If it is my will that he remain until I come, what is that to you?"*

This is the disciple who is testifying to these things and has written them, and we know that his testimony is true. But there are also many other things that Jesus did; if every one of them were written down, I suppose that the world itself could not contain the books that would be written.

To contemplate:

Even the disciple that Jesus loved
    had to die to enter life.
Yet before his death he testified
    to the things that are written here.

No, the world of books cannot contain
    the things that Jesus did.
The whole wide world cannot contain
    the Jesus who is Christ.

O John, beloved of Jesus Christ,
    and spiritual son of Mary,
thank you for witnessing to his life;
    thanks for telling his truth.

O Jesus Christ, the Word of God,
    beloved Son of the Father,
thank you for coming down to us
    and dying on Calvary.

Thank you for sending us from the Father
    your own Holy Spirit,
to guide us on our way to you
    and be our Advocate.

We pledge to you our heart and soul,
    our mind and loving will.
With Peter and John and all the rest,
    we promise to follow you,
follow you till your kingdom come
    and we rest in it with you!

Dear John,

Beloved disciple of Jesus Christ,
   you who best knew his heart,
and even rested your head on his breast,
   thanks for revealing his love!
Listening there upon his breast
   to the heartbeat of your Lord,
you truly believed he was God-become-man
   to save us from our sins.

From the day the Baptist called him Lamb,
   Isaiah's Lamb of God,
you followed him all through Galilee,
   on up to Jerusalem.

From Cana to Samaria to Bethany
   you observed his greatest works;
you witnessed all the signs he gave
   of his true identity.

You listened to the human words
   of the very Word of God,
and in your heart you pondered them,
   interpreted them for us.

The words the synoptics relay to us
   have a deeper inner meaning

that you, more than any other witness,
　　caught and translated for us.

You followed him on his way to death,
　　stood by him on Calvary,
received his mother into your home,
　　cherished her as your own.

And you saw him after his resurrection
　　when he brought his disciples peace,
and when he prepared a meal for them
　　on the day they caught no fish.
You heard him ask Peter for his love
　　and brace him to bear his cross;
and through the years you held his words,
　　pondered them in your heart.

Dear Jesus,
O Jesus of the Gospel of John,
　　revealer of God's own words;
O Word of God, become a man,
　　you bring God's love to us!

You teach your disciples to follow you,
　　find who you really are;
you show them your zeal for your Father's house,
　　and response to your mother's word.
You teach Nicodemus the way to life,
　　to life within the Spirit.
You teach the Samaritan woman to yearn
　　for the living water of grace.

You forgive a woman caught in sin,
    you give sight to a man born blind;
you heal a man on the sabbath day,
    though you scandalize the righteous.

You raise your friend Lazarus from the dead,
    though you must give your life for his;
you wash the feet of your disciples,
    though you know they'll abandon you.

You tell your disciples of your Father and Spirit,
    and of your abiding love;
You let soldiers arrest you in the garden,
    despite your superior strength.

You stand before Pilate and the crowd,
    bear all their infamy;
your carry your cross for love of us,
    all the way to Calvary.
And finally you forgive us all,
    empower disciples to forgive;
you encourage Peter to declare his love,
    for you have loved us first.

BOOKS & MEDIA

The Daughters of St. Paul operate book and media centers at the following addresses. Visit, call or write the one nearest you today, or find us on the World Wide Web, www.pauline.org

CALIFORNIA
3908 Sepulveda Blvd., Culver City, CA
90230; 310-397-8676
5945 Balboa Ave., San Diego, CA
92111; 619-565-9181
46 Geary Street, San Francisco, CA
94108; 415-781-5180

FLORIDA
145 S.W. 107th Ave., Miami, FL
33174; 305-559-6715

HAWAII
1143 Bishop Street, Honolulu, HI
96813; 808-521-2731

ILLINOIS
172 North Michigan Ave., Chicago, IL
60601; 312-346-4228

LOUISIANA
4403 Veterans Memorial Blvd.,
Metairie, LA 70006; 504-887-7631

MASSACHUSETTS
Rte. 1, 885 Providence Hwy.,
Dedham, MA 02026; 781-326-5385

MISSOURI
9804 Watson Rd., St. Louis, MO
63126; 314-965-3512

NEW JERSEY
561 U.S. Route 1, Wick Plaza,
Edison, NJ 08817; 732-572-1200

NEW YORK
150 East 52nd Street, New York, NY
10022; 212-754-1110
78 Fort Place, Staten Island, NY
10301; 718-447-5071

OHIO
2105 Ontario Street (at Prospect
Ave.), Cleveland, OH 44115;
440-621-9427

PENNSYLVANIA
9171-A Roosevelt Blvd., Philadelphia,
PA 19114; 215-676-9494

SOUTH CAROLINA
243 King Street, Charleston, SC
29401; 843-577-0175

TENNESSEE
4811 Poplar Ave., Memphis, TN
38117 901-761-2987

TEXAS
114 Main Plaza, San Antonio, TX
78205; 210-224-8101

VIRGINIA
1025 King Street, Alexandria, VA
22314; 703-549-3806

CANADA
3022 Dufferin Street, Toronto, Ontario,
Canada M6B 3T5; 416-781-9131
1155 Yonge Street, Toronto, Ontario,
Canada M4T 1W2; 416-934-3440

¡Libros en español!